CHAOS
2 CALM

the moms-of-multiples' guide
to an organized family

CHAOS 2 CALM

the moms-of-multiples' guide to an organized family

TONIA TOMLIN

Sorted Out™

Plano, TX

Sorted Out Publishing
An imprint of Sorted Out™
2124 Deerfield Drive
Plano, TX 75023

For more information regarding special discounts for bulk purchases, please
contact Sorted Out at 972-985-7515 or orders@momsofmultiplesguide.com.

A goodmedia communications, llc book.
Book design by Blu Sky Media Group
Illustrations by goodmedia communications, llc
Book cover design by Gwyn Kennedy Snider
Cover photo by Andy Netzer of Netzer Photography
Author Photo by Gittings Photography

The text in this book is set in Adobe Garamond Pro & Minion Pro

Manufactured in China

10 9 8 7 6 5 4 3 2 1

Library of Congress Cataloging-in-Publication Data

Tomlin, Tonia
Chaos 2 Calm/Tonia Tomlin – 1st Edition • p. cm.
Library of Congress Control Number: 2008900562

Summary: An organizational guide for preparing a couple's marriage, home,
life and family for new twins, triplets or quadruplets.

1. Multiple birth. 2. Child rearing. 3. Parenting.
I. Title. II. Title: Chaos to calm.

HQ777.35.T66 2008 • 649'.144 • QBI08-600011

ISBN-10: 0-9801548-0-4
ISBN-13: 978-0-9801548-0-1

To my mothers, Pat Cote for teaching me organization and being consistent with me from the moment I was born; Mavis Wedel for keeping me organized during high school; Patricia Tomlin for taking care of me during the most difficult part of my life.

To my Father for believing in me and sharing with me his entrepreneurial spirit.

To my loving husband for giving me the encouragement to write this book.

And, to my two beautiful twin babies, Peyton and Sydney.

TABLE OF CONTENTS

Prologue

Chapter 1

A New Way of Life.. 1
The Joy of Journaling 1
It Takes Two 2
Team Work 3
Togetherness Tips.. 4
Parents Who Partner Together, Stay Together 5
Division of Household Chores 5
Family Core Values 6
Dollars & Sense 7
Doctor Bills.. 8
Diapers 9
Diet 9
Seek Out Support 10
Be Wary Of Borrowing 11
Freebie Requests.. 12
Action Tips 16
Be Consistent.. 17
Additional Resources.. 17
Forms.. 19

Chapter 2

Creating Space For Babies 31
Baby Placement.. 31
The Nursery 32
The Sleeping Zone 33
The Changing Zone 34
The Play Zone.. 36
The Mommy & Me Zone 37
The Closet.. 38
The Bathroom 39
The Kitchen 40
The Communication Center 40
The Family Room 41

Chapter 3

Creating a Baby Safe Space.. 45

Carbon Monoxide.. 46

Smoke Alarms 46

Hot Water.. 46

Fire Escape Ladder 46

Fire Extinguishers... 47

First Aid Kit... 47

Cabinets.. 47

Blind Cords 48

Furniture... 48

Electrical Outlets.. 48

Doors.. 49

Doorstops 49

Gates.. 49

Fireplace.. 49

Kitchen 50

Freezer Fresh 51

Bathrooms 53

Nursery... 53

Additional Resources... 54

Facts About Injuries to Children at Home........................... 54

Chapter 4

Easy Etiquette 57

Showers, Sip & Sees and Christenings 57

Shower Shoulds & Should Nots.. 57

Sip & Sees... 58

Christian & Secular Christenings.. 59

Additional Resources... 60

Forms.. 61

Chapter 5

Childcare Challenges.. 67
The Nanny Search... 67
Hiring Nanny 68
She Is Like Family 68
The Nanny Employee Handbook............................... 69
Family Orientation 71
Daycare 71
Steps to Choosing a Daycare 72
Additional Resource.. 73
Forms.. 74

Chapter 6

Nest & Rest 95
Nesting No-Nos.. 95
Mom's Hospital Bag.. 96
Partner's Hospital Bag.. 96
Babies' Homecoming Bag 96
Rest & Readiness 96
Bed Rest (less·ness) 97
Surviving Bed Rest In The Hospital 97
At-Home Bed Rest.. 98
Additional Resources... 99

Chapter 7

Homecoming.. 101
Getting settled into a new way of life 101
Tips For Preparing Your Singletons For Multiples 102
Breastfeeding Your Babies...................................... 103
Diaper Duty... 105
12-Steps to Disposable Diaper Changing 106
Folding Cloth Diapers... 107
Steps to Cloth Diaper Changing Using a Wrap 107
Steps to changing a cloth diaper using pins 108
Be a Delegating Diva.. 109
Connect To Your Calm Place 110
Additional Resources.. 111
Forms.. 112

Chapter 8

Routine, Routine, Routine 115

Feeding 116

Sleeping 116

Activities 117

Sign Up For Signing 117

Additional Resources 118

Forms 119

Chapter 9

The Terrific Twos Times Two 123

Turn The Terrible Twos To Terrific Twos! 124

Help Your Toddlers Help Themselves 125

Additional Resource 125

Chapter 10

Mother Nature's Baby 127

Eco-Friendly Baby Food 129

Eco-Fashion For Mommy & Baby 130

Eco-Play 131

Keeping It All Eco-Clean 131

Eco-Playground 132

Additional Resources 133

Chapter 11

Babies On The Go 135

Babies' First Wheels 135

Diaper Bag Checklist 136

Parents' Guide To Traveling With Multiples 138

Carry-On Diaper Bag 139

Eliminating Ear Pain 139

What To Pack & What To Purchase 140

Epilogue

Resources

Forms

Index

Quick Order Form

Acknowledgments

I would like to thank the following families and individuals for their generous participation in the preparation of Chaos 2 Calm. Without their dedication, editorial criticism, and friendship, this book would have never moved beyond the "idea phase." Thank you for your support and for inspiring me to continue with this dream and goal of mine! I love you all.

Rob, Peyton and Sydney Tomlin—Rob for your honest feedback and to my babies, this is for you! Thank you for being patient with me.

Pat Cote—where do I start? My mother, you have taught me a vast majority of what it means to be a great worker, as well as a wonderful mother to my twins. You are my inspiration. Thank you for always believing in me. Ray Wicker—Dad, thank you for inspiring and developing my entrepreneurial spirit. Thank you for your honesty and for teaching me to treat others how you want to be treated.

Patricia Tomlin—you have always been my best friend, thank for encouraging me to continue with the book and for your endless supply of great ideas.

Mavis Wedel—my other mother—thank you for always indulging my obsessions for white hangers when I was in high school. I still don't do wire hangers!

Kristi DeWall—your wisdom and advice have helped me through some of the toughest moments in my life; I will never be able thank you enough for being there for me.

Robyn Short, goodmedia communications—you are an amazing writer, editor and friend, I love you girl! Michael Albee, goodmedia communications—your imagination is amazing. Thank you for sticking with me.

Ashley and Andy Netzer, Netzer Photography—you both did a tremendous job dealing with four babies on the set, I can't thank you enough.

Jack, Alicia, Taylor and Jackson Maxwell—Whew! What a wild ride. Thanks for listening to me when I needed you the most. We appreciate you being a part of this project.

Donna Smallin-Kuper—your expertise and feedback have been appreciated so much. Thanks for all your quick responses and honesty.

Jack Smith—Baby Proof USA—we love all your products, thanks for your participation in this amazing adventure.

Christy Ilfrey, our native mommy, thank you for your contribution and for being the visionary that you are in making our world a greener place to bring up our next generation.

To Diana San Roman, Michael Preston—thank you for putting up with me!

Maryglenn McCombs—I couldn't ask for someone more honest, and team-orientated as you. Thank you for your guidance and making this project big hit!

Rarely does a woman's professional career actually prepare her for her role as a mother, but that is exactly what I had unknowingly been preparing for in my career as a professional organizer.

It has been said that sales people are born and not made, and there may be some truth to that. Organizing is much the same; some of us have an innate knack for understanding and developing systematic processes that improve efficiency and flow—the flow of a workspace, a home, a project and even a way of life.

A well-organized person communicates efficiently, works efficiently, manages her time efficiently and creates a lifestyle of processes that make change and transitions manageable and even pleasant. My organizing business, Sorted Out™, was born from my entrepreneurial spirit and highly marketable talent for simplifying people's lives through organizational processes.

Sorted Out is a professional organizing company that helps corporations and individuals save time, money and even relationships by establishing a well-organized system of processes. I am a member of the National Association of Professional Organizers (NAPO), and through this association with NAPO, I was discovered by HGTV's Mission: Organization.

My involvement with Mission: Organization was a truly great experience. The show provided unlimited resources allowing the Sorted Out team to create the most functional and organized space that literally changed the lives of the family we organized.

Time and again I have watched my clients lives change from chaos to calm, as their dysfunctional space became a well-organized space that supported them rather than drained them. Their communication changed, their experiences with one another changed, and their attitudes shifted as their lives became more organized. And I realized how blessed I was to be apart of this amazing transformation day in and day out.

When my husband and I were blessed with our twin daughters, I became aware of the challenges moms-of-multiples are faced with each day. Through my relationships with various moms, I witnessed first-hand how a lack of organization can wreak havoc on moms-of-multiples in every aspect of their lives, from their daily routines to even their relationships with their partners. In my own life, I was faced with the challenge of taking my own organizational processes, within the home and in my personal and professional life, up a notch. Parenting multiples is like living life in the fast lane where there literally is no rest for the weary.

It is my hope that this book will be a guiding light for you through your pregnancy and beyond. Within these pages you will find suggestions, tips and advice to help you maximize your time, organize your home, life and relationships, and develop processes to prevent chaos and disorder. You will be amazed at what a powerful impact organization can have in your life.

Chapter 1

A New Way of Life

"We're having a baby!"
These four words will change
your life forever.
But, nothing compares
to the other four words,
"Congratulations!
You're having multiples!"

Like most moms-of-multiples, the moment I learned I was carrying two babies I experienced an overwhelming rush of emotions: excitement, intrigue and absolute astonishment. And, like most dad's of multiples my husband experienced sticker shock! Visions of double everything flashed in his head: car seats, cribs, highchairs, tricycles, and bicycles … the list goes on and on. And yet, with the rush of emotions and flashing dollar signs, there is no sweeter moment. From that moment on, I knew we were in for a new way of life.

THE JOY OF JOURNALING

If you have never kept a journal before, this is the time to start. The experience of having living, growing human beings inside of you is such a fascinating and emotional experience. The process of journaling will help you establish a deeper bond with your babies, as well as with your spouse. Begin journaling with your spouse, as well as separately, as early in your pregnancy as possible. You will want to record your complete experience. Be consistent and selective when journaling. Discuss your feelings, emotions, physical and mental changes, as well as what may seem like ordinary details, as you will look back on this time fondly some day. There are many reasons why it is important to record this time in your life.

1. Journaling will assist in developing an early relationship with your babies while you are pregnant.
2. Journaling with your partner or spouse will allow the two of you to establish a stronger relationship, as well as bring your one another into the experience in a more intimate way.
3. You will be experiencing a rush of new emotions all the time. Keeping a record of this experience will be insightful to reflect on during and after the pregnancy.
4. Journaling will help you to remember the details of your pregnancy that would have been lost over the course of time.
5. Your children will understand you and themselves better later in life when they have the opportunity to read the journal themselves.

Most importantly, understand why you are journaling and what you hope to gain from it. This will help you as you record your experiences.

IT TAKES TWO

Having just one baby will change your way of life. Having more than one baby will turn your life upside down, and shake it around. There is no way of knowing the intricacies of how these new human beings will impact your relationship with your spouse, but you can bet it will change in one way or another. I cannot stress the importance of consciously and deliberately creating "us" time in the early months of your pregnancy. If your multiples are your first children, you will never have this much time together again.

The journey the two of you are about to embark on will challenge and test your relationship in ways you could never imagine. In the early months of your pregnancy, relish your time together. Go on as many date nights as possible. When you are tired, have a special date night at home.

Once you establish the habit of making date night a part of your relationship, keep this routine after the babies are born. You may have to have more at-home dates, but the time together will be essential to keep your bond as a couple strong. If possible, plan to have at least two vacations a year, one with the children and one as a couple. Get creative with your vacation options in order to address your budgetary limits. Time away from home can be expensive, but the time together is priceless.

TEAM WORK

Parenting multiples requires a particularly strong partnership and commitment to working together. Communication and clearly defined expectations are essential to the success of your relationship as parents, as well as your relationship as partners. Organization is key in developing and maintaining a system that works for both you and your spouse.

Spend time in the early months developing an organizational structure outlining expectations for partnering together. You may want to hire a professional organizer, lifestyle and relationship coach or counselor to assist you in this process. There are many important considerations that should be agreed upon prior to the arrival of your babies.

TOGETHERNESS TIPS

FIRST TRIMESTER	SECOND TRIMESTER	THIRD TRIMESTER
Take your last vacation as a couple together: a cruise, mountain get-away, the beach, etc.	Spend the weekend at a local hotel and pamper yourself and each other.	At-home holiday: turn off the phones & email. Enjoy a spa weekend at home together with no distractions from the outside world.
Friday night out at the movies: enjoy your babysitter-free cinema while you can!	Purchase a DVD set of your favorite TV shows & have a standing weekly TV-Dinner movie night.	Rent a day's worth of movies and stay in bed together watching movies and eating popcorn.
Schedule Sunday brunch at a nice restaurant and then enjoy an afternoon symphony.	Create a five-star picnic in your backyard together with candles and homemade ice cream.	Spend an evening massaging each other's hands & feet while you daydream about your new life together.
Write a letter to each baby together. Share your hopes and dreams for each baby.	Spend an evening going through photos together of your courtship, wedding & honeymoon. Create a scrapbook for your children to enjoy.	Create a time capsule containing something from every date during your pregnancy to open together in ten years.
Take a camera out with you for the day and shoot fun candid photos of the two of you at the park, museum, water gardens, etc.	Have a professional photo shoot of the two of you as parents-to-be.	Purchase a sculpting kit and spend an evening at home creating a mold of mommy-to-be's belly.
Take a cooking class together.	Cook dinner together and create a fine dining experience at home with your china and crystal. Linger over dinner and enjoy each other's company.	Daddy-to-be prepares breakfast in bed and the two of you eat and spend the morning snuggling together.
Spend an evening creating an "I-owe-you" card box filled with romantic promises to be redeemed during & after your pregnancy.	Take a bubble bath together. Light candles and indulge in one another's company.	Find a book you both enjoy and spend an evening snuggling on the sofa reading to each other.
Start a family Web site together and create an online journal with photos of your pregnancy that you can update as your family grows to together.	Stargazing ... Plan a day trip to an out of the way place where you can have an evening picnic and enjoy gazing at the stars into the evening.	Purchase a Questions For Couples book (or create your own) and spend an evening learning new things about one another.

PARENTS WHO PARTNER TOGETHER, STAY TOGETHER

In any cohabitating relationship the issue of who does what domestic chore is sure to come up. If you have not yet had that conversation with your spouse, now is the time to do so. And if you have had that conversation, now is the time to revisit it.

Successful parenting is truly a joint partnership. While one parent can do it all, two is certainly optimal. Parenting multiples is a challenge unlike any other. Parents must function as one unit in unison with one another in every way.

Both parents need to closely evaluate their schedules. How the responsibilities unfold will be different for everyone, but the conversation must take place prior to the babies' arrival. This will not only allow for you to have an open and honest conversation about the division of household and parenting responsibilities, but it will also be a tremendous assistance in understanding what additional help you may need from friends, family and/or hired help. You will most definitely need additional help in the first two years of your children's lives.

Sample forms are included in this book to assist you in creating a schedule that will address your unique circumstances. Forms for your personal use are included on the CD you received with this book. Be sure your conversation with your spouse includes the following:

DIVISION OF HOUSEHOLD CHORES (INSIDE & OUT)

- You will have more laundry than you ever thought possible. How will this chore be divided?

- Is it necessary to hire a housekeeper or gardener?

- Work schedules and realistic work hours (i.e., working late hours may need to be addressed, as well as travel schedules).

5

- Will one parent stay home? If so, that will impact the distribution of household responsibilities.

- Will you hire a nanny? What will her household responsibilities entail?

- If you will be utilizing daycare, who will drop off and pick up?

- Do you have friends or family that will be willing to help out regularly?

- Who will do nighttime feedings? Early morning feedings?

- Who will prepare bottles? Should you do it in the morning or evening?

These may seem like questions that will naturally sort themselves out as they are presented. They may naturally sort themselves out, but chances are the division of labor will be inequitable, and eventually that inequity will take a toll on the relationship. A fair division of chores makes for a healthy parenting relationship while providing the children with the opportunity to know both their parents as caregivers.

FAMILY CORE VALUES

If you have not yet discussed your family's core values with your spouse, now is the time to do so. You may even want to enlist the service of your minister or family counselor, as their professional expertise will be beneficial in guiding the conversation and leading you down paths of discussion that you may not arrive at on your own. Use the Family Core Values form provided with this book as you create the guiding principles for your growing family.

As you work on this project together, keep in mind that your spousal relationship, and the way in which you hold your relationship sacred—or not—will be the pinnacle of the family unit. Your relationship will be the model that will have a lasting impact on how your children perceive and experience relationships within their own lives. If you want your children to treat you and each other with respect, you must model this behavior at all times between each other.

DOLLARS & SENSE

If you did not create a budget prior to your pregnancy, do it now. The cost of birthing and raising multiples can be overwhelming if financial planning is not established from the very beginning.

While there are many costs associated with raising multiples to adulthood, the three major expenses that will impact the first two years of your children's lives are what I call the "Three Dollar-Ds": Doctor Bills, Diapers and Diet.

Good to Know

Cutting Back On Couture: 10 Tips For Low-Cost Finds

1. Buy clothing out of season. Stores always discount clothing to make room for next season. Buy now for next year.

2. Shop consignment stores. Most consignment shops cater to high-end clothing. You will need to get over the desire to dress your babies exactly alike, but that is probably a good thing. You can find some fantastic selections if you are willing to dig through the racks.

3. Clear out the clearances. Put your blinders on when shopping retail and head straight to the clearance racks.

4. Checkout the outlet malls. Brand named stores at outlet malls often sell the previous season's offerings at greatly discounted rates.

5. Go part-time. If you can't resist buying this season's cutest couture, consider taking a part-time job at your favorite store. The babies can go to Mothers' Day Out, and you will probably enjoy the "quiet" time.

6. Good Will hunting. Seriously, you can find some cute things at the Good Will if you look hard enough. And, you will be putting your money towards a good cause as well.

7. Watch out for closeouts. Keep an eye out in newspapers, on TV, on the radio and as you drive around for clearances and closeouts.

8. Buy quality not quantity. Cheap clothes are not synonymous with a good value. Buy the previous season's discounted quality items over the current season's cheap stuff.

9. Stay in the know. Chat with other moms, and read up on mom Web sites to stay in the know of what stores are having closeout sales and when.

10. Get friendly with eBay. Hone your tech skills and get savvy on eBay and other online auction sites.

> Successful Parenting is truly a joint partnership

DOCTOR BILLS

With sixty percent of twins and ninety percent of higher order births occurring within the first 37 weeks of gestation, it is much more likely there will be additional medical costs associated with your children's arrival than with a singleton baby. And, when carrying quadruplets and quintuplets, it is pretty much a guarantee that the babies will arrive prematurely. As a matter of fact, the average gestation for quintuplets is only 29 weeks. With the heightened risk of pre-term labor, along with other common multiple-birth complications such as Preeclampsia, placental dysfunction and twin-to-twin transfusion syndrome, there is also a very high chance of a pre-birth hospital stay that may last for weeks or even months.

Our pregnancy was no exception. Twenty-two weeks into our experience I was diagnosed with twin-to-twin transfusion syndrome (TTTS). TTTS is a disorder of the placenta in which one baby (the recipient) has more blood and amniotic fluid than the other baby (the donor). This is caused by a difference in the blood pressure of identical twin babies who share a placenta. The blood has a tendency to flow to the baby with the lower blood pressure, leaving the donor baby with higher blood pressure with less blood. TTTS is most often seen in monochorionic, diamniotic twins and affects an estimated 6,000 babies a year. If the disorder begins in the first two trimesters, it is likely that one or both of the babies will not survive without medical interference. An estimated 80% of babies affected by TTTS do not survive, largely due to failure to diagnose or adequately treat the problem.

Delivery by cesarean is very common with multiple birth deliveries, which will also result in additional inpatient recovery time. Premature babies require in-hospital care for weeks or even months.

Early financial preparation is essential. For example, our medical bills exceeded one million dollars prior to insurance payment. With our insurance covering 80% of our in-network expenses, we were left with a substantial balance to be paid out of pocket. Because we did not utilize fertility treatment for our pregnancy, our twins—and the costs associated with them—were a complete surprise. Fortunately, we budgeted several years in advance for parenthood; the money was just spent differently than we anticipated.

DIAPERS

On average, you can expect to use about 70 diapers per week, per child in the first several months of your babies' lives. While they will use less as they age, the size of their diapers, and therefore the cost, will increase. If you choose to use disposable diapers, expect to spend about $10 per child per week on diapers. So, for twins you could budget about $80 per month, triplets $120 per month, etc.

Of course, there is also the option of cloth diapers, which is easier on the pocketbook and the planet, but not so easy on a parent's already chaotic lifestyle. According to research conducted by the Real Diaper Association, a generous selection of pre-folded diapers and diaper covers can be purchased for about $300–$1000 depending on whether you choose organic cotton, fitted diapers and wool covers or standard cotton.

Over the course of three years, disposable diapers will cost an estimated $5,760 for twins while cloth diapers will cost an estimated maximum of $1000 for both children. Families with higher order births will spend significantly more.

DIET

Whether you are breastfeeding, formula feeding or a combination of both, you can expect your grocery bill to increase significantly. In the first year of life, babies are sustained on primarily breast milk or formula. You may find that you are more reliant on formula than you originally intended simply because your body is incapable of producing the volume of milk your babies require. Or, you are incapable of meeting the time restraints required to breastfeed or pump for two or more babies.

If you are strictly feeding your babies formula, expect to spend about $30 per week, per child ($120 per month, per child). If, and when, you switch the babies to cow's milk or soy milk, you should budget for two gallons of milk per child, per week and one gallon of juice per child, per week.

Good to Know

If you plan to purchase diapers in advance, only purchase about three to four weeks worth of pree-mie diapers, as your babies will grow out of them surprisingly quickly. Be sure to save your receipts so you can exchange your diapers if necessary.

Ask your friends and family to purchase gift cards in lieu of diapers for shower gifts.

Become a bargain shopper. Clip coupons, buy in bulk and always take advantage of sales. You may even qualify for government support. To find out more information for government programs visit www.fns. usda.gov/wic/.

See the sample budget for an itemized look at the expected costs for the first two years of your babies' lives. A budget form is provided on the accompanying CD for your personal use.

SEEK OUT SUPPORT

As soon as you learn that you are pregnant with multiples, seek out support from local organizations such as Mothers of Multiples or the National Mothers of Twins Club. The purpose of these organizations is to create a space for support, exchange of knowledge and ideas, and to provide a forum for mothers to receive education and a sense of community. Get involved as early into your pregnancy as possible so you have the support from mothers who have been in your situation and can advise you from first-hand experience. You will also receive valuable information about what to expect when your babies arrive.

Most likely you will spend some time on bed rest before your babies arrive. Begin making arrangements for that possibility as soon as possible. While it may be hard to ask your friends and family to do laundry, grocery shop and prepare food, retrieve the mail and all the other nuances of daily life, you will have to have the help, especially if you already have children.

It is not too soon to begin calling and scheduling help for post-pregnancy. While you may not know exactly when your babies will arrive, you will have a general idea. Get used to asking for help. Your friends and family will want to help, but they need your direction to know how to help.

Use the Sign-Up to Assist form to help you fill in all of the time gaps in which you will need help. Make sure to have a couple of people willing to be on stand-by in case your scheduled assistant is not able to make it.

BE WARY OF BORROWING

When you announce to your friends and family that you are pregnant, and especially when you announce that you are pregnant with multiples, a beautiful thing happens—generosity rains down on you in abundance. However, while generosity is almost always well intended, when it comes to borrowing or accepting an unsolicited loan, there are some guidelines that should be strictly adhered to. And, absolutely never ask to borrow an item. If you would like to borrow something from a friend, wait until an offer is extended.

Once you announce your joyful news, friends and family often begin offering maternity clothes, baby clothes and baby equipment. Sometimes it is offered as a loan and sometimes as a gift. If you choose to accept, always assume it is a loan, and do not accept anything you do not actually need. The most well intended gift, can easily cause hurt feelings based on misunderstandings, and/or miscommunications or damage to the gifted item. Keep the following in mind when you accept a gift or a loan from a friend.

- Always assume it is a loan even when presented as a gift.

- Accept it only if you are willing to replace it if it is damaged or broken.

- Return the item in the same condition (or better) than you received it.

- If you are borrowing clothing, get detailed instructions on how the garment should be laundered.

- If you stain the garment, replace it with something comparable or give a gift certificate.

- If you don't want it, don't accept it.

- Whether you accept it or not, send a thank you note for the offer.

- Return the item as soon as you no longer have a use for it.

- If the item was presented as a gift, offer it back when you no longer need it. If the person who

Good to Know

The Twins Network is a great place for learning about new studies, twin events, interesting facts, as well as a place to blog with other moms-of-multiples. www.twinsnetwork.com

Many of the moms-of-multiples groups have a Single Support Coordinator to assist moms-of-multiples who are parenting without a spouse or partner. If you are a single parent, be sure to utilize this resource.

It is not too soon to begin calling and scheduling help for post-pregnancy gave it to you insists it was a gift, ask if you may donate it to charity or send to a consignment store. Get your friend's approval before discarding the item. If she does not want you to discard of it, insist that she take it back—you then know that it was a loan not a gift.

PRIOR TO DELIVERY

Write letters to the following companies requesting samples of their products. Once your babies are born, attach a copy of your babies' birth certificates to the letters and mail them. You will be delighted by the many free products you will receive!

BABIES "R" US offers 10% off two or more of the same item purchased in the same order. For example, two cribs, two bedding sets, two strollers. The discount is only good for categories such as furniture, bedding sets, and baby gear. Baby gear includes car seats, strollers, travel yards, highchairs, swings, gates, exersaucers, walkers, and backpack carriers. www.babiesrus.com.

BEECHNUT BABY FOODS Call 1-800-233-2468 to request a free "new parents' pack" for twins, triplets, or quads.

CARNATION Join their new birth program and receive $20 in free products. 1-800-811-7500

> Carnation Good Start Formula
> Nestle Infant Nutrition
> PO Box AW
> Wilkes-Barre, PA 18703

CARTERS Carters' offers are available for triplets and higher order births only. Send copies of birth certificates to the following address:

> Carters
> Attn: Multiples Birth Program
> 224 N. Hill St.
> Griffin, GA 30223

DRYPERS Join the new birth program and receive free packages of Drypers and coupons. Must provide letter and birth certificates.

AFP
PO Box 8830
Vancouver, WA 98666-8830

EARTH'S BEST FOODS For the Earth's Best Family Program call 1-800-442-4221. They will send you coupons on a regular basis by enrolling in their program.

ENFAMIL Call them to receive formula coupons.
1-800-222-9123

EVENFLO Call 1-800-233-5921 to receive a free gift basket for parents of multiples. You will need to include copies of birth certificates.

Evenflo
1801 Commerce Drive
Piqua, OH 45356

THE FIRST YEARS This program requires a letter and copies of birth certificates for free merchandise such as rattles, teething towels, etc.

The First Years
Attn: Multiples
1 Kiddie Dr.
Avon, MA 02322

GERBER Call 1-800-443-7237 to sign up for the Gerber Multiple Birth Program. You will be required to send copies of birth certificates.

Gerber
Attention: Multiple Birth Program
445 State St.
Freemont, MI 49413

HEINZ Call 1-800-872-2229 to receive a free welcome packet for twins, triplets or quads.

HUGGIES Send proof of birth to the following address. Huggies will send you coupons for diapers and wipes.

> Kimberly Clark Corporation
> Dept. QMB
> PO Box 2020
> Neenah, WI 54957-2020

JC PENNEY PORTRAITS Complete the online form and register for the Multiple Birth Program. Portrait coupons will be listed via email and through the mail.
www.jcpenneyportraints.com/multiples

JOHNSON AND JOHNSON Call 1-800-526-3967 to receive free coupons for their baby products.

MCNEAL CONSUMER PRODUCTS The makers of Tylenol will send coupons for their goods. 1-800-962-5357.

OCEANSPRAY Receive a special assortment of coupons by mailing in a copy of your babies' birth certificates.

> Ocean Spray Cranberries, Inc.
> One Ocean Spray Drive
> Lakeville-Middleboro, MA 02349

OSHGOSH B' GOSH They offer 10% discount on apparel at most clothing stores. Ask for the store manager to apply the discount.

PAMPERS OR LUVS Call 1-800-726-7377 to request free products.

PROCTOR AND GAMBLE Call 1-800-285-6064 to request coupons for your multiples. Also ask to join their mailing list.

RINGLING BROTHERS BARNUM & BAILEY CIRCUS Sign up online for free tickets to the Circus. You must attend before your twins, triplets or quads are one. www.ringling.com/offer/baby. After registration, print out the forms and send copies of birth certificate to:

Baby's First Circus
Feld Entertainment, Inc.
8607 Westwood Center Drive
Vienna, VA 22182

ROBEEZ Call 1-800-929-2649 or go to www.robeez.com and email their customer service department. They will give you a 10% discount on each pair of shoes for your multiples.

SIMILAC Call 1-800-232-7677 for free samples. Also ask your pediatrician to ask for free samples of formula for your babies.

TINY LOVE Tiny Love® offers parents and families of multiples the Multiple Births Program. This program offers buy one-get-one free on all Tiny Love products purchased directly through (888) TINY-LOVE number. To qualify, please send a completed MBP Qualification Form (http://www.tinylove.com/data/uploads_EN-US/pdfs/MBP_Qual_Form.pdf), along with proof of the births or expected births, such as birth certificates, via fax or mail to:

Fax: (714) 898-7945
E-mail: customerservice@mayagroup.com
Post Mail: Tiny Love/The Maya Group, Inc.
Attn: Multiple Birth Dept.
12622 Monarch St.
Garden Grove, CA 92841

WAL-MART FIRST CHOICE FORMULA Call 1-866-877-9177 to receive one free can of formula.
Write them a letter telling them about the birth of your babies along with a birth certificate.

PMB Product Inc.
204 N. Mail
Gordonsville, VA 22942

WHITE HOUSE GREETING This offer is not twin specific, but very cool! Send a letter to the President regarding your babies' birth and you will receive a personalized letter from the President. I actually did this and put it in the babies' scrapbook. My husband thought it was the coolest thing ever!

The White House Greeting Office
Room 39
Washington DC 20500

ACTION TIPS

1. Create a Mommy & Babies Medical Binder or purchase the MyPRO™ Health Records Organizer and include the following in each of the binders.

   - Explanation of Benefits (EOBs)
   - OBGYN contact info
   - Pediatrician contact info
   - Hospital information
   - Test results
   - Copies of medical bills
   - Payment receipts of all medical expenses
   - Cord Blood Kit

2. Ask your doctor for sample products that have been provided by various companies. This will help you determine what products are best for you before making a purchase.

3. Write to all of the companies whose products you would like to try. Most companies have a policy of sending samples to new moms.

4. Purchase a coupon organizer that easily fits in your purse. Keep this with you at all times.

5. Create a call list for delivery. Designate one person to call friends and family.

BE CONSISTENT

- Develop a Partnership Plan and be dedicated to fulfilling it.
- Be committed to your date nights.
- Journal often—at least weekly.
- Develop your budget and live by it.

FORMS

- Partnership Plan
- Family Core Values
- Sample Budget
- Sign Up to Assist
- Request For Samples Letter

ADDITIONAL RESOURCES

- Baby to Bee is a Web site every expecting parent should utilize. Download coupons, get freebies, get advice on current products and receive helpful tips. www.babytobee.com
- Planning Family offers free samples, product offers, coupons, and sweepstakes from well known brands. www.planningfamily.com
- Order discounted diapers (and much more) and receive free shipping from www.diapers.com.
- Mr. Rebates (www.mrrebates.com) offers a vast variety of home and baby products. Every purchase earns you cash back.
- From birth announcements to strollers, Just Multiples offers a wide variety of products specifically for parents of multiples. www.just multiples.com
- BabyCenter.com provides helpful tips and general month-by-month expectations for pregnancy.
- The National Organization of Mother of Twins Club, Inc. www.nomotc.org

- MOST (Mothers of Supertwins) is a wonderful organization that provides support to "Multiple Birth Families ... Every Step of the Way." www.mostonline.org

SUGGESTED READING

- Twice Upon A Time: Twin baby memories by Lynn Lorenz

- Expecting Multiples DVD Course: DVD 1 Preparing for Multiples with Nutrition & Preventative Care; DVD 2 - The Birth Experience & Life with Multiples

- Sweet Jasmine, Nice Jackson - What It's Like To Be 2-And To Be Twins! by Robie H. Harris and Michael Emberley

- Subscribe to Twins Magazine as soon as you learn you are pregnant with multiples. www.twinsmagazine.com

- Twin to Twin by Margaret O'Hair and Thierry Courtin

- TwinsTalk.com is a great resource for parent-to-parent advice.

PARTNERSHIP PLAN

The purpose of the Partnership Plan is to form a commitment between you and your spouse to fairly and lovingly assign specific household chores to one another. As you create your partnership plan, keep in mind the division of labor can and should be revisited as your lives evolve and change.

DAILY CHILD CARE

Duty	Monday	Tuesday	Wednesday	Thursday	Friday	Saturday	Sunday
Early Morning Feedings	mom	dad	mom	dad	mom	dad	mom
Late Night Feedings	dad	mom	dad	mom	dad	mom	dad
Morning Bottle Prep.	mom	Nanny	Nanny	Nanny	Mom	Grandma	Grandma
Late Night Bottle Prep.	both	both	both	both	both	both	both

DAILY HOUSEHOLD CLEANUP

Duty	Monday	Tuesday	Wednesday	Thursday	Friday	Saturday	Sunday
Kitchen Cleanup							
morning	mom	nanny	nanny	nanny	mom	grandma	grandma
noon	mom	nanny	nanny	nanny	mom	grandma	grandma
evening	both	both	both	both	both	both	both
Laundry							
children's	mom	nanny	nanny	nanny	mom	grandma	grandma
adult	mom	nanny	nanny	nann	mom	grandma	grandma
Beds							
children's	mom/nanny	nanny	nanny	nanny	mom	mom	mom
adults	nanny	nanny	nanny	nanny	mom	mom	mom
Meal Prep.							
breakfast	mom	mom	mom	mom	mom	grandma	grandma
lunch	mom	nanny	nanny	nanny	mom	mom	mom
snack	both	both	both	both	both	both	both
dinner	both	nanny	nanny	nanny	both	both	both

PARTNERSHIP PLAN

The purpose of the Partnership Plan is to form a commitment between you and your spouse to fairly and lovingly assign specific household chores to one another. As you create your partnership plan, keep in mind the division of labor can and should be revisited as your lives evolve and change.

	Duty	Monday	Tuesday	Wednesday	Thursday	Friday	Saturday	Sunday
WEEKLY HOUSE-HOLD CLEANUP	Lawn Care						dad	
	Pool Care				Pool Company			
	Grocery Shopping	both		both		both		

Special Considerations
Should we hire a housekeeper? If so, how many days per month should he or she work?
Yes, we are going to hire a housekeeper. Once a week for the first three months, when the babies are little. Then after three months we will move to every other week. We would like the house keeper to come on Tuesdays.

Discuss your current professional work schedule. Are there adjustments that need to be made with regard to the number of hours worked or the amount of travel required?
We will work our professional schedules around what the babies needs are and plan to hire a part-time nanny. With Grandma's help on the weekends this will help out with the other duties that need to be completed. Also, we will communicate with our employers to make the transition easier for the children. We will make the request to have light travel in the first three months.

Will one parent stay home with the children long-term? How will this impact the division of labor?
One Full-Time, to obviously cover medical benefits and other benefits from the company. One Part-Time to keep active in the work force. The division of labor will be divided as we see fit. We will use the reciprocity rule in our house for sure!

Will you hire a nanny? What will her household responsibilities entail?
Yes, we will hire a nanny for part-time work. The main responsibilities will be to help with the babies' care and keeping up with laundry, dishes and the normal maintenance of a household. Dinner, lunch and other meals will be a big part of the responsibility especially when mom is breast feeding.

If you will be utilizing daycare, who will drop off and pick up?
For now we won't be utilizing day care, but will consider it an option when mom goes back to work full-time.

Do you have friends or family that will be willing to help out regularly?
Yes, grandma is willing to help on the weekends for the first three months. After that, it will be as needed.

FAMILY CORE VALUES

The purpose of the Family Core Values form is to commit on paper what you and your spouse agree will be the core governing principles of your family. Your core values should be what structures every important family decision. You should be able to ask yourselves prior to making a decision: Will this support our family's core values? A simple yes or no answer to that question should be all you need to move forward with your decision.

Your family's core values should ...
- Govern your personal inter-family relationships
- Guide your home processes
- Clarify who you are as a family unit
- Articulate what you stand for as a family
- Be a parental guide for teaching your children
- Be a parental guide for rewarding your children
- Provide a moral foundation for the family

Together, with your spouse or any other children who may currently reside within the family, develop a two to three sentence statement for each of the following prompts:

Our family will hold the following virtues as the guiding principle for all inter-family relationships:

 __We will strive to teach our children consistency by leading by example. Our marriage__
 __comes before our children. Respect others and the environment around you.__

The following principles will be the foundation of all our home processes:

 __Be honest, contribute to the household, always appreciate each other & what we have.__
 __You only have one family.__

As a family, we will continuously strive to be:

 __Open with communication, treat others with respect.__

As a family, we will make a stand for our most sacred truths, which are as follows:

 __There are no secrets. If we have something to say, we would like to bring it out into the__
 __open. If one has an issue we will try to bring it up as soon as possible.__

FAMILY CORE VALUES

The purpose of the Family Core Values form is to commit on paper what you and your spouse agree will be the core governing principles of your family. Your core values should be what structures every important family decision. You should be able to ask yourselves prior to making a decision: Will this support our family's core values? A simple yes or no answer to that question should be all you need to move forward with your decision.

As parents, we agree to support one another in our effort to educate and morally guide our children by implementing the following method of discipline:

__We will always think about the consequences before we react to you. We will provide__
__age appropriate discipline measures. We will always be a good role model for you.__

_____

_____

As parents, we agree to support one another in our effort to educate and morally guide our children by implementing the following reward system:

__We must tell you three times a day when you are doing something great and reward__
__with love and limited material objects. We will also commit to one on one with mommy__
__and daddy as a reward.__

_____

As parents, we promise one another that we will mutually commit to providing the following moral foundation for our children:

__We will always lead by example. i.e.. No TV when we are eating as a family. We will__
__show you we care about you by setting limits on external variables that change__
__families day in and day out.__

_____

Additional:

_____
_____
_____
_____
_____
_____
_____
_____
_____
_____
_____
_____

SIGN UP TO ASSIST

Use the Sign Up To Assist form to ensure you have ample help on hand when your babies arrive.

	Time	Monday	Tuesday	Wednesday	Thursday	Friday	Saturday	Sunday
DAILY HOUSEHOLD CLEANUP	7:00 am							
	7:30 am							
	8:00 am							
	8:30 am							
	9:00 am	Jan		Jan		Jan		
	9:30 am							
	10:00 am							
	10:30 am							
	11:00 am	Teri	Teri	Teri	Teri	Teri		
	11:30 am	Teri	Teri	Teri	Teri	Teri		
	12:00 pm							
	12:30 pm							
	1:00 pm							
	1:30 pm							
	2:00 pm	Heather	Heather	Heather	Heather	Heather	Heather	Heather
	2:30 pm							
	3:00 pm							
	3:30 pm							
	4:00 pm							
	4:30 pm							
	5:00 pm	Teri	Teri	Teri	Teri	Teri	Teri	Teri
	5:30 pm							
	6:00 pm	Grandma		Julie	Julie		Grandma	Grandma
	6:30 pm	Grandma		Julie	Julie		Grandma	Grandma
	7:00 pm							

SAMPLE LETTER

Your Name
Your Address
Your City, State, Zip
Your Email

Date

Name
Address
City, State, Zip

To Whom It May Concern:

Please find enclosed copies of our twins' birth certificates. We know you can imagine the cost involved with having twins and we appreciate any complimentary products your company may be able to offer. We would also appreciate any coupons, so we can purchase your goods in the future.

Sincerely,

Your Name Here

SAMPLE BUDGET
MONTHLY EXPENSES

PERSONAL CARE	MONTHLY COST	KITCHEN	MONTHLY COST	BATHROOM	MONTHLY COST
DIAPERS	$80.00		$		$
WIPES	$10.00		$		$
DIAPER RASH CREAM	$7.00		$		$
MYLICON	$7.00		$		$
BREAST PUMP	$45.00		$		$
PACIFIERS	$		$		$
PAIN RELIEVER MEDICINE	$5.00		$		$
MEDICATION	$		$		$
MEDICATION	$		$		$
MEDICATION	$		$		$
	$		$		$
	$		$		$
	$		$		$
	$		$		$
	$		$		$
	$		$		$
	$		$		$
	$		$		$
	$		$		$
	$		$		$
	$		$		$
	$		$		$
SUB TOTALS:	$154.00	+	$	+	$
=					
TOTAL	$154.00	X 36 MONTHS =		GRAND TOTAL	$5,544.00

SAMPLE BUDGET
ONE-TIME EXPENSES - A

PERSONAL CARE	ONE-TIME COST	KITCHEN	ONE-TIME COST	BATHROOM	ONE-TIME COST
FIRST AID KIT	$ 30.00	BOTTLES	$ 64.00	SPOUT COVER	$ 3.00
HUMIDIFIER	$ 30.00	BOTTLE WARMER	$ 18.00	4 - HOODED TOWELS	$ 20.00
BODY SUPPORT PILLOW	$ 60.00	STERILIZER	$ 90.00	12 WASH CLOTHS	$ 20.00
MILK STORAGE BAGS	$ 10.00	SIPPY CUPS	$ 24.00	INFANT TUB	$ 15.00
TOWELS	$ 10.00	FLATWARE/CUTLERY	$ 7.00	BATH MAT	$ 10.00
		PLATES/BOWLS	$ 10.00	POTTY CHAIR	$ 27.00
		BOTTLE DRYING RACK	$ 6.00		
		BOTTLE BRUSH	$ 4.00		
		CABINET LOCKS	$ 30.00		
		6 BIBS	$ 20.00		
		HIGH CHAIR	$ 100.00		
		BOOSTER SEAT	$ 30.00		
		12 -BURP CLOTH	$ 16.00		
SUB TOTALS	$ 160.00	+	$ 419.00	+	$ 95.00
=					
TOTAL A	$ 674.00				

CAR	ONE-TIME COST	NURSERY	ONE-TIME COST	PLAY STATIONS	ONE-TIME COST
INFANT SEAT	$ 100.00	CRIB	$ 230.00	BOUNCY SEAT	$ 35.00
TODDLER	$ 219.00	MATTRESS	$ 100.00	EXER-SAUCER	$ 60.00
CAR ROLLER SHADE	$ 15.00	MATTRESS PAD	$ 20.00	BUMBO SEAT	$ 40.00
CAR MIRROR	$ 15.00	4 PC BEDDING SET	$ 150.00	ACTIVITY PLAY MAT	$ 60.00
SEAT SAVER	$ 22.00	EXTRA CRIB SHEET	$ 20.00	SWING	$ 90.00
		2 SHEET SAVERS	$ 16.00	EVENFLO JUMP-N-GO	$ 40.00
		MOBILE	$ 50.00		
		CHANGING TABLE	$ 160.00		
		CHANGING TABLE PAD	$ 22.00		
		2 CHANGING TABLE PAD COVERS	$ 40.00		
		5- RECEIVING BLANKETS	$ 10.00		
		BABY BLANKET	$ 20.00		
		BOPPY	$ 25.00		
		BOPPY COVER	$ 12.99		
		DIAPER CHAMP	$ 30.00		
		NIGHT LIGHT	$ 5.00		
		SLEEP-TIME POSITIONERS	$ 10.00		
		HAMPER	$ 20.00		
SUB TOTALS	$ 371.00	+	$ 940.99	+	$ 325.00
=					
TOTAL B	$ 1636.99				

TRAVEL	ONE-TIME COST	SAFETY	ONE-TIME COST
STROLLER	$ 140.00	OUTLET PLUGS	$ 8.00
BJOURN	$ 100.00	DOOR KNOB COVER	$ 8.00
DIAPER BAG	$ 40.00	4- SECURITY GATES	$ 120.00
PACK AND PLAY	$ 100.00	MONITOR	$ 70.00
SUB TOTALS	$ 380.00	+	$206.00
=			
TOTAL C	$ 586.00	A+B+C= GRAND TOTAL	$2,896.99

Monthly Exp Grand Total*	$5,544.00
One Time Exp Grand Total	+ $2,896.99
Grand Total	= $8,440.99
Singleton Cost	$8,440.99
Twin Cost	$16,881.98
Triplet Cost	$25,322.97
Quad Cost	$33,763.96
Quint Cost	$50,645.94

Please note, Monthly Expense Grand Total is based on 36 months.

Chapter 2

Creating Space For Babies

*While you can certainly prepare your home for your babies'
arrival without the assistance of a professional organizer,
the best advice I can give for the purging and planning
aspect of preparing for your babies' arrival is to employ a
professional. This process can be very daunting for some
people. So much so, it is easy to let this aspect of preparation
go until it is too late. Because I was placed on bed rest early
in my pregnancy, my friends and family created my nursery
for me. By bringing fabric and paint swatches, catalogues
and décor ideas to the hospital to consult with me, I was
able to be part of this wonderful and sentimental process.*

BABY PLACEMENT

As the mommy, you will quickly learn to recognize each of your children based on the
little nuances of their physique and personality. However, it will take other caregivers,
aunts and uncles, friends longer to pick up on the individuality of all the children. In
order to prevent confusion, develop a baby-placement system. If you have twins, place
Baby A on the right side and Baby B on the left side in all situations. For example, Baby
A's crib is on the right side of the room, while Baby B's is on the left side of the room.
Baby A's highchair is on the right, and Baby B's is on the left. The same goes for the car
seat, photo shoots, etc. For higher birth orders, create a similar system of placement. Also,
assign a particular color to each child. For example, Baby A always wears clothing that is
predominantly lavender, Baby B wears yellow, etc. This will be a great help for your friends
and family as they develop their own relationship with your little ones. As time goes on,
you will know when this process is no longer necessary.

THE NURSERY

The first step in planning for your babies' nursery is to decide on the space. What room will be used for the nursery? Once you have decided on the space, you must determine what you will do with the furniture and items that are currently occupying that space. Go through the room as well as the closet and eliminate everything in the room that you no longer use or need. Label four boxes: Trash, Recycle, Donate and Storage. Place the items you are eliminating in one of these four boxes.

You may decide that converting the master suite to the nursery makes more sense and will be more practical for your babies (especially if you have three or more) while they are all sharing a room. If—or when—the children move into their own rooms, you can move back into the master suite. The goal is to create a space that will be the most practical, and ultimately the most convenient for you.

Second, remove the furniture. Re-locate the furniture to somewhere else in the house, place it in storage, sell on eBay or Craig's list, or give it away. Freecycle.org is a great site for unloading furniture or other items you no longer want or need. Be honest with yourself about the value of the items you are removing. If you really have no use for it, get rid of it. Get the room and closet pared down to a clean slate.

Third, create an Interior Design Organizer or purchase one. I use the MyPRO™ Interior Design and Decorating Organizer, which is available at www.SortedOut.biz. The purpose of your interior design organizer is to assist in the collaboration of your color scheme, fabric, paint, wallpaper, flooring and linen swatches, as well as all other décor items. Your organizer should include folders for swatches, design pages, a section for notes, a section for tear sheets, contact information, coupons, etc. Take this organizer with you on each of your shopping trips so that you readily have all of your design elements available to you when making purchasing decisions. This organizer will prove invaluable to you as the children are older and you need to make improvements to their rooms that require the detailed information you have organized and stored within your organizer.

Preparing a nursery for multiples is quite different than preparing for singletons. In a singleton pregnancy, it is reasonable to put off decorating and preparing the nursery until your seventh or eighth month or even post-pregnancy. You will not want to wait if you are carrying multiples. As discussed in the previous chapter, you will most likely have a significantly shorter gestation period, and you may spend a good portion of your pregnancy on bed rest. Your post-pregnancy time will be stressful as you transition to your new life and new sleeping pattern. You will want to have everything prepared as early as possible to ease the transition into your new lifestyle as a parent of multiples.

Another difference in preparing a nursery for multiples is that you will need to have one child (or children) in a safe place while tending to each individual child. The best way to accomplish this is by dividing your nursery into separate zones: a sleeping zone, changing zone, play zone and a "mommy and me" zone.

THE SLEEPING ZONE

There are varying opinions about whether multiples should co-bed or each have their own crib. Your decision may largely be made by the space available in the room dedicated as the nursery. Some parents may even consider preparing separate nurseries; however, I caution against this. Separate nurseries will double or even quadruple your expenses and will have you running all over the house trying to care for the children. Also, you will probably find that your babies want to be together. So, in this book, we will only discuss a single-room nursery.

If you choose to co-bed, you will need to save space in your nursery for an additional crib (or more if you are a parent of triplets, etc.). As the babies grow, they will need more space in which to move and sleep. Also, you will probably have a difficult time separating the children when it is time to utilize multiple cribs. If you do choose to co-bed your babies, the Sleep-Time Positioner by www.EspeciallyBaby.com is a great product to help your babies stay on their side of the bed.

It is wise to provide an individual crib for each baby from the get-go. Shop consignment stores, yard sales, eBay and Craig's list for used cribs. While you will want to purchase new mattresses, you will definitely want to save money on this piece of furniture, as you will only be using them for about three years. Do not worry about finding exact matches, you can utilize different styles and paint them in similar themes. As a matter of fact, you may find that you prefer different styles for your children so that you can allow for individualization from child to child, and additional décor interest. Remember to place your cribs in the proper order (Baby A on right, Baby B on left).

There are several considerations to keep in mind when determining the best placement for the cribs. You will want to protect the babies from direct sunlight. You may want to have access to the nursery while the babies are sleeping, so placing the cribs a distance from the door is smart. And, the babies will find comfort, as they age, in having visual access to one another, so parallel placement is better than headboard to footboard.

THE CHANGING ZONE

As a parent of multiples, you will quickly learn the importance and necessity of multi-tasking. Opting for a dresser-style changing table versus a traditional changing table serves several purposes. One, with multiple children, you will want to take every opportunity to save on expenses. Utilizing a dresser as a changing table and adding diaper-changing pads to the dresser top will allow you to convert this piece of furniture into a functional dresser that the children will be able to use as they age. By hanging shelves in the changing station for diapers, lotion, powder, etc., you can utilize the drawers for the clothing basics: pajamas, onesies, casual clothes, socks and hair accessories. Second, a dresser-style changing table is long enough to allow for two changing stations on top so that when help is available, two children can be changed at the same time.

You will need several organizational bins and drawer liners that fit your dresser drawers. Use the bins to hold socks, hair accessories, extra diapers and wipes (unless you have these stored on nearby shelving).

You will want to position the changing station so that you have visual access to the rest of the room rather than having it against the wall with your back to the room. You can accomplish this in two ways: Simply place the dresser with the drawer side facing the wall so you can stand behind it and face towards the room while working. You can hang shelves on the wall behind the dresser. Or, place the changing station in a corner flush to a wall with the drawer side facing the wall so that it creates a cubby-like space. This position is actually preferable as you will be able to hang shelves and perhaps a diaper bag on the sidewall with easy access to all the essentials.

Hang a mobile or other decorative item from the ceiling over the changing table so that the baby has something to play with and contemplate while having her diaper changed. This will assist in a quicker and cleaner diaper change, as her attention will be focused up rather than on her dirty, bare bottom.

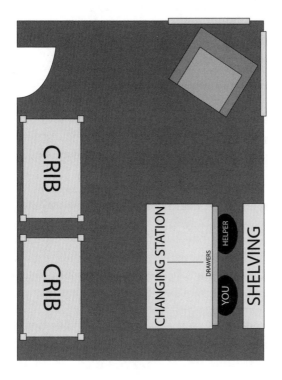

Option 1

Simply place the dresser with the drawer side facing the wall so you can stand behind it and face towards the room while working. You can hang shelves on the wall behind the dresser.

Option 2

Place the changing station in a corner flush to a wall with the drawer side facing the wall so that it creates a cubby-like space. This position is actually preferable as you will be able to hang shelves and perhaps a diaper bag on the sidewall with easy access to all the essentials.

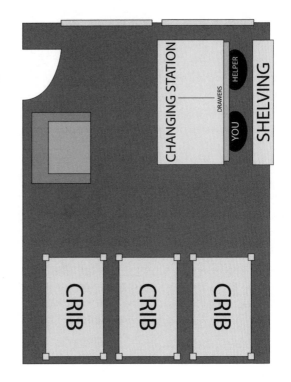

CHANGING STATION

DRAWERS

HELPER

YOU

SHELVING

CRIB

CRIB

CRIB

THE PLAY ZONE

The play zone should be in easy view of the changing table. Develop a system of either placing the babies in their cribs while changing the children one at a time, or as they age, prepare a simple play zone where you can easily see the children while your hands are tied with the baby in the changing station.

The play zone should be simple, clean and have limited toys. Children function best when they have limited options. By placing everything your babies own in a toy box in the room, they become overwhelmed and are consequently challenged to focus on or enjoy any one particular item. Limit the toy selection to one per child, plus one. For example, if you have twins, place three items on a toy shelf that is within the child's reach. For triplets, place four toy choices. Be sure that each of the toys is somewhat similar in function to reduce sibling bickering. For example, don't have a battery-operated car as a choice and two puzzles. The car will be the source of bickering.

When the children are small, replace each toy on the shelf prior to changing each child. As they age, teach your children to replace the toy themselves prior to being changed. This will teach them respect for their belongings, but it will also reduce quarrelling as the toy will have been replaced and made available for another child to play with (after he has replaced his toy, of course!).

THE MOMMY & ME ZONE

The mommy and me zone is where you will place your rocking chair and other comfort accoutrements for the little ones. You will need a small side table or chest with enough storage space for your breast pump, wipes, reading material for yourself to enjoy when pumping, towels for spills, a lamp, burp cloths and several children's books. If you have the space, a small refrigerator is very helpful. When the children are still babies you will want to include a comfort item for each child less one (the child you are rocking) such as a bouncer, swing, doorway jumper, BeBe Pod or Bumbo Babysitter or any other item that can keep each child physically occupied and safe while tending to the baby or babies you are rocking. As your children age, you may want to replace these items with individual rocking chairs where they can sit and rock their own babies or "read" a book while waiting for their "mommy and me" time.

Unless you want to be a slave to the washing machine, you will have—and need—more blankets than you can possibly imagine. Your children can easily use two per child each day. You will want blankets and burp cloths to be quickly and easily accessible. Your mommy and me zone is the best place to store these items. Choose two wicker baskets or bins that are in keeping with your nursery décor to always have a ready supply on hand.

The mommy and me zone is a good place to spend one-on-one quiet time with each child. While they may all have cohabited in your womb, they each want to know you individually and to be loved and experienced as individuals. By having at least thirty minutes per day with each child,

Good to Know

Check out www. easyexpression.com 1-866-522-7177, for a selection of must-have hands-free pumping bras for the multi-tasking mommy of multiples.

Just as your children will frequently outgrow of their clothing, they will also "outgrow" their toys. Make a habit of purging your children's toys at the same time that you purge their clothing. I also recommend purging both clothing and toys prior to your children's birthdays, as well as prior to major holidays.

you will develop a special bond with each of your children outside of the "multiple unit." This individual bond will prove invaluable to you and your children as you all function as a family.

THE CLOSET

Tackling the closet early is important. You will definitely want this space prepped and ready to go when gifts and loaner clothes start pouring in. Along with a clean slate to work with, you will need the following:

- Three large, airtight, clear, plastic bins with a place for labels, plus one additional bin per child.

- Hanging size-dividers

- Built-in shelving

- Hanging shoe rack

Utilize your plastic bins to store clothing the children have outgrown. Keep three bins on hand at all times and label them in six-month increments. In the first two years of growing, you will find that your children are often between sizes. They may be wearing 0–3 months in some brands and 3–6 months in another. Also, your children may not always wear the same size as their siblings.

Keep a labeled storage bin in the children's closet. As the children outgrow their clothing, wash it, fold it and pack it away in the bin. Decide what you want to do with the clothes they can no longer wear. You may want to save it for future children; if so, remove the garments from your children's closet and store it in an appropriate place. You may choose to give the items away to friends, sell them on eBay, take them to a consignment store or donate them. Do not allow yourself to fill more than three bins without purging. Three is manageable, but more than three is overwhelming. If you choose to sell your clothes on eBay or through consignment, you will get a better price for your clothes if they are purchased just prior to the season in which they should be worn.

As you empty or store the bins, either re-label them or replace them, and place them back in the closet for the next round of outgrown clothes.

Purchase one bin per child and label it with his/her name. Use this bin to store sentimental items that are specific to that child. You will want to keep these bins in the closet or under the child's crib or bed (if you have a bed/crib skirt) so that you have easy access to it and can easily save items as needed.

Purchase size-dividers to hang in the closet. Buy these in three-month size increments. Sort your clothing first by size, then by category (pants, tops, dresses, skirts, etc.) and then by color. If you have identical sets of various outfits, be sure to hang them side-by-side. Keep at least two size increments in the closet at all times, so that as your children outgrow their clothes, new, clean outfits are readily available to replace them. By keeping two sizes in the closet at all times, you will also be able to assess what their clothing needs are for the next stage growth and prepare accordingly.

If you do not already have built-in shelving, install a shelving unit in the closet. Purchase at least six bins that will fit on the shelves for accessory items such as hats, headbands, gloves, scarves and other garment accessories.

Place a door-hanging shoe system with pockets so that each pair can be stored together in a pocket. The best shoe systems have mesh pockets, which allow the shoes to "breathe." Again, this will keep the closet clean, but will also provide a visual for keeping up with inventory and assessing future needs.

THE BATHROOM

Designate a particular bathroom that will be used exclusively for the children. It is easy to utilize one bathroom for everyone, but you will be truly grateful to have a "grown-up" bath that is used exclusively for the grown-ups. We all need a relaxing place that is our own where we can go to de-stress from a hard day. The bathroom is often that place. Let your bath be your own personal sanctuary by keeping the rubber ducks and strawberry shampoo in the children's bathroom.

A clean and orderly bathroom is essential for efficiency,

PRODUCT PICK

Knock Knock has a clever and convenient Take Out Menu Organizer includes 30 sleeves for storing up to 60 menus, six tabbed-dividers for various cuisines, 50 ratings stickers, takeout tips and a 50-sheet group-ordering pad. Check them out at www.knockknock.biz

PRODUCT PICK

I recommend Pottery Barn's Daily System. This system is designed to be compatible with all of the latest technological gadgets. This system incorporates Smart Technology—a built-in six-plug cord-set—which keeps your families' electronic devices organized and easily accessed. This modular system is designed as single unit with whiteboard on one side and storage cubbies with a power cord on the other. The letter bin doubles as a magazine rack. Check out the complete system at www.potterybarn.com.

but more importantly, it is essential for safety. Place a rubber mat on the bottom of your porcelain tub to minimize the risk of slipping. As your children age and continue bathing together, bath time can get rowdy. Keep the tub as safe of a place as possible. Purchase a faucet cover (they come in all kinds of fun characters) to protect your children's heads from unexpected clashes with the metal faucet. Place all toys in a net bag that suctions to the wall and enforce the clean-up rule prior to exiting the tub to prevent tripping. The bag will also allow the water to drip from the toys and dry naturally, which will reduce the growth of bacteria. Store all of your children's towels and washcloths in the cabinet closest to the tub. Always have a dry bath mat for the children to step on when they are old enough to climb out of the tub independently.

Every item that is child safe, or that your children can use independently, should be stored in a place where they can reach it. Create a space that never requires a child to climb on a counter top in order to exercise his independence. Keep the drawers and cabinets in the bathroom free of any cleaning supplies or other toxic agents. The children's bathroom should be designed to be a total safety zone.

Establish this space as a safe, child proofed space from day one. Your life as a parent of multiples is very hectic and your children will grow and become independent much more quickly than you realize.

THE KITCHEN

As a parent, you will spend a lot of time in the kitchen. Consequently, your children will too. Once your babies are old enough to crawl, create a cabinet and a drawer exclusively for them. Choose a cabinet that is out of the way of the flow of traffic, as well as the sink, oven and microwave. Keep toys, plastic ware, wooden spoons, etc. in the cabinet and drawers for them to play with. By redirecting them to their cabinet each time they come to the kitchen, they will quickly learn that this is their designated place.

Designate a cabinet exclusively for the babies' bottles, nipples, bottle lids, pacifiers, and cups with lids. You may also want to store the formula in this cabinet if space allows. You will definitely find that prepping bottles ahead of time makes feeding much more efficient. Reserve half of one shelf in your refrigerator for bottles. Allow for one row per child and label that row with the child's name. This way you can identify to whom each unused or unfinished bottle belongs. This is very important to prevent the spread of colds or other illnesses. Your children may also be on different formulas and this system will prevent confusion. Designate a specific shelf in the pantry exclusively for the children's pantry items: rice, cereal, baby food, powder or canned formula, teething biscuits, etc.

The kitchen is the best place to store your children's medication. Keep everything in a small portable, plastic tote that you can easily transport and that easily fits in the cabinet.

THE COMMUNICATION CENTER

Every well organized home should have a communication center. This is an area set up in a high-traffic area such as the kitchen, mudroom, home office, etc. I recommend the kitchen, as this tends to be where all facets of communication take place. The communication center should have a designated space for all of the following items: mail, cordless phone, mobile phone power dock, iPod power dock, camera power dock, a calendar, note pads or "to-do" and "to-buy" lists, homework, clock, pens and keys. The communication center is a one-stop location for all of your daily communication needs.

THE FAMILY ROOM

Your home should be comfortable for everyone living in it, but that does not mean you have to live in a toy wonderland. Designate a specific closet or armoire for your children's toys. Keep only the toys that are currently age appropriate within your child's reach. Limit the number of toys they have available for free play, but rotate them out frequently. By having limited choices, your children will be able to better enjoy and focus on the task at hand, and will consequently take better care of their things. The same rule should apply here as in the Play Zone in the bedroom: one toy per child, plus one.

The family room should have the same accommodations as the mommy and me station in the nursery: bouncer, swing, doorway jumper, BeBe Pod or Bumbo Babysitter and one or two playpens depending on the number of multiples you have. My recommendation is one playpen per every two children.

If your home is two level or larger than 2000 square feet you should include a baby changing station in the family room. This station does not need to be as elaborately stocked as the nursery but should contain all of the essentials: a changing pad and cover, wipes, diapers, diaper rash cream and powder. Again, having a mobile hanging above the changing station is beneficial, but for your family room you may opt for something simpler like a stuffed animal or other soft toy.

In order to maintain a sophisticated décor, you may want to get creative with how the changing station is displayed. With the popularity of plasma TVs, many people have an entertainment system with a TV tray that is no longer being used. Secure a changing pad to the tray, place all the changing essentials in baskets or bins and when you are finished changing the diapers simply slide the tray back into the unit and close the door. The same can be done with an armoire.

Chapter 3

Creating a Baby Safe Space

By Jack Smith, CEO of InfantHouse.com

"The greatest potential threat to the average American child is that child's own family and home environment."
- C. Everett Koop, Former U.S. Surgeon General

Before starting our business, my wife and I were blessed with twins. We took our responsibility very seriously when it came to baby proofing; however, we made a lot of mistakes due to lack of information. There are a lot of products on the market and some of the most popular and least expensive are not very good. Thankfully, we avoided any unintentional baby proofing injuries, and we discovered a market for baby proofing homes for others.

Multiples present challenges to baby proofing that singletons do not. Parents of multiples are going to have more than one child exploring and neither of them know better. The following are just some of the challenges parents of multiples are faced with:

- Multiples can move in two different directions; you move in one.

- Even if they are in the same room, you potentially can only see one at a time.

- Two toddlers are stronger than one.

Also, multiples will have the opportunity to injure each other; whereas, a singleton can only injure herself. For instance, instead of having a pinched finger from a cabinet door for a singleton, you may have a more severe injury from a sibling closing the door on the other's finger.

The kitchen is the heart of the house. Parents spend a great deal of time in the kitchen even when not preparing meals. If you decide you would like to have one or two child-friendly drawers—drawers created with items specifically for your children to play with—be sure to utilize a drawer or cabinet that is well out of the way of traffic, the oven, stove, microwave and refrigerator.

The best place to begin is with an in-home professional consultation. This is a room-by-room tour through the home with one of the parents. We use an extensive, eight-page checklist to survey our clients' homes.

An overall home recommendation is to remove or secure all heirlooms for a period of time to avoid damage. If possible, move these items as well as other knickknacks out of reach of the children. Not only does this save your belongings, but it also limits the number of times you have to say "no." As a simple example, change any stone coasters to rubber, and thereby save the coaster and your wood furniture from damage.

The best way to discuss baby proofing a home is to "walk" with me through each room or area. Some of these items pertain to the entire home, while others are more room specific. There will be descriptions after each item to better explain.

CARBON MONOXIDE

If the home has gas appliances or fireplaces, check for carbon monoxide detectors. The recommendation is one per story, and each monitor should be wall-mounted.

SMOKE ALARMS

At a minimum, smoke alarms should be installed near the bedrooms and near the kitchen. The best solution is to have one inside and outside every bedroom.

HOT WATER

The water heater needs to be set to 120 degrees Fahrenheit to prevent scalding.

FIRE ESCAPE LADDER

At a minimum, multi-level homes should have one two- or three-story fire escape ladder. Store the ladder in the youngest child's room, as he or she is the most helpless. Older children should be better able to follow your instructions in the event that the home needs to be evacuated. If you have multiples, and they are in the same room, then one ladder will be sufficient. If they are in separate rooms, you may need to consider having a ladder for each room.

Implement family fire drills periodically so as to prevent panic should you ever actually have a fire. If there are multiple small children, this will be your opportunity to practice whom is responsible for each child, and how best to evacuate. Do not actually use the fire escape ladder during the drill; this will prevent potential injury from falling.

FIRE EXTINGUISHERS

The recommendation is one fire extinguisher per level of the home. This may give you the time you need to evacuate. Always remember, your first priority is to evacuate the home and call for help, not to extinguish the fire.

FIRST AID KIT

Keep one first aid kit in the kitchen where you have water, towels, ice and a phone. This makes clean up much easier and you avoid mirrors that can be a distraction for facial injuries. For multiples, you may want to consider having a safe play area where you can put the one(s) not being attended to at the time. This keeps your full attention on the injured child.

CABINETS

You should lock all drawers and cabinets below the counter top regardless of the contents to prevent poisoning or burns from cleaning solutions or other chemicals, as well as pinched fingers or worse. Be careful which latches you choose, as some allow cabinets and drawers to be opened slightly. While your children may not be able to remove any items, they can still get their fingers hurt. The best solution is to use the Tot Loks™ by Safety First. These latches will not allow the drawers or cabinet doors to open without using the magnetic key, which is easily placed out of reach by the parent. An added benefit is that these latches may be turned off when they are not needed and easily turned back on when necessary. This is beneficial for a grandparent's or caregiver's home where the children visit only on occasion.

BLIND CORDS

Most parents will raise the blinds up so children can look outside and also to avoid potential damage to the blinds from a curious baby. When you raise the blinds, the cords should be secured up and out of a child's reach to prevent strangulation. Secure the cords in a permanent manner and not just tossed up on top or hidden behind the blinds. Blind cord cleats or the Blindwinder™ from KidCo are both excellent solutions for this issue.

FURNITURE

Secure all pieces of furniture over three-drawers high to the wall to prevent injury. If a child were to open all of the drawers on a chest, the center of gravity shifts to the front and could topple over, injuring the child. The best and strongest straps are the furniture wall straps from Safety First. They need to be installed into a stud in the wall and then to the back of the furniture. Do not forget about your televisions, they also need to be secured to prevent them from falling. There is a TV strap available to secure smaller TVs. Use two straps for larger units. With multiples, securing these items is even more important. For example, one child can be climbing on the furniture or TV and cause it to fall while the other one is under it at the time.

ELECTRICAL OUTLETS

All outlets below the counter top need to be secured to prevent electric shock or worse. One of the most popular items to do this is an outlet plug. Unfortunately, these are easily pulled out by your child and pose an additional choking hazard. These plugs actually add a concern to your life instead of eliminate one. The best solution is to switch out your existing plate covers with a spring-loaded sliding electrical plate. These are very easy for adults to use, but difficult for children to manipulate.

Surge protectors and outlet strips are a hazard as well, and the little orange/red light is a baby magnet. Use a power strip cover to secure this hazard. While the items above protect you from the most dangerous concern—electrocution—there are other items that can make your life less stressful such as plug and adapter covers, as well as cord shorteners.

DOORS

Doors leading outside or to dangerous rooms need to be secured. Most parents prefer to use a door top lock. This device slides on the door itself and hooks around one screw in the top of the door frame. The lock can be operated from either side of the door. We also recommend these, as younger children are able to figure out how to use the typical plastic doorknob cover.

DOORSTOPS

A favorite pastime of babies is flicking the coiled doorstops. They are at their level, and we all know they make a great sound. While noticing the wonderful sound, babies will also notice that the soft cap on most doorstops is removable. This is a leading cause of choking in infants. Remove these doorstops, and replace them with a one-piece doorstop.

GATES

Gates are recommended at the top and bottom of stairs until your children reach 24-months of age or until your child is able to open it or climb over the gate. Hardware-mounted gates are needed for stairs, as they are the most solid. Pressure-mounted gates can be easily pushed over especially with more than one child doing the pushing. Most gates are removable, and it is best to leave the hardware installed until the youngest child is four years of age in case there are issues with sleepwalking. There are a lot of different gates on the market. Gates from KidCo meet the highest safety standards, and they can be modified to fit any situation from simple doorways to a fireplace and staircases. Metal gates are easiest to clean and stay looking nicer longer. They are available in black or white.

FIREPLACE

For a raised hearth fireplace, a gate is a great option to avoid injuries from the hearth, as well as from the heat. This also prevents the children from finding choking hazards inside the fireplace such as "lava rocks" and small pieces of unburned wood. The ashes can also be hazardous if they are stirred up and inhaled.

KITCHEN

This area of the home has an incredible amount of traffic, and there are potential hazards that are not in other rooms. In addition to locking the cabinets and drawers that has already been discussed, the stove, oven and burners need to be secured as well to prevent burns.

Ground Fault, GFI, outlets should be installed within six feet of all sinks and other water sources to prevent electrocution. The dishwasher should be secured as it usually has the utensil basket containing sharp objects on the bottom within easy access of toddlers, and the coil gets hot enough to melt plastic as well as burn skin.

Trash compactors, ice machines and wine refrigerators need to be secured. Refrigerators should be secured to keep toddlers out of medicines and alcohol. Also, glass bottles and jars are easily broken on the hard surface, kitchen floor.

Kitchen bar stools seem to be a popular place to hang a purse, and with a simple tug the stool will usually tip over. It is best to remove the bar stools to prevent them falling over when a toddler starts climbing.

All toys should be in another room to avoid trip hazards. Most parents want to secure the pantry door to prevent grazing and the potential injuries from climbing, broken jars and broken toes from dropped items.

Good to Know

Is this safe to it eat? Busy moms know the value of leftovers and pre-prepared meals. Quick eats can be a lifesaver during the week. Use this guide to know just how long you can safely hold onto your leftovers. Be sure to label and date anything you put in the freezer or the refrigerator.

Freezer Fresh

Fish, meat and uncooked poultry:

- Ground beef should be consumed within four months of freezing.
- Beef chops should be consumed within six months.
- Roast and steaks are good up to one year in the freezer.
- Fatty fish such as salmon should be consumed within three months, while leaner fish such as sole and flounder should be consumed within six months.
- Whole chicken can be kept frozen for one year, but chicken pieces should be consumed within nine months.

Frozen Dinners should be tossed after four months.

Frozen Veggies can be safely consumed within one year.

Ice Cream has a short life and should be thrown away once it gets ice crystals or after one month.

Leftover Stews & Casseroles should not be kept longer than three months. Be sure to label and date all leftovers.

Nuts can actually go rancid pretty quickly. If you do not eat them within a month, wrap them tightly and store them in the freezer. Keep salted nuts up to eight months and unsalted nuts up to one year.

Bread should be consumed within three days of purchasing. If you do not plan to eat it all that quickly, wrap it tightly and keep in the freezer for no more than three months.

Fridge Fresh

Baby food: An open jar of fruit or veggies is safely consumed within two days.

continued...

Cheese: Remove the plastic the cheese is wrapped in and rewrap it in wax paper with plastic wrap around the wax. Keep cheese indefinitely, but cut out any mold that develops and one additional inch beyond on all sides. Wash the knife between slicing to ensure cleanliness.

Condiments: Adhere to the expiration dates on all condiments. Do not keep an open jar of mayo longer than two months.

Eggs: Keep eggs deep in the back of the fridge where it is coldest, and use within three to five weeks of purchase.

Raw seafood and raw ground beef: These meats should be consumed within one to two days.

Chops, roast & steaks: These raw meats should be consumed within three to five days.

Bacon: Raw bacon is good for one week.

Deli meats: Deli slices are good for three to five days.

Poultry: Chicken should be consumed within one to two days.

Jams & Jellies: Adhere to the expiration date and toss upon any signs of mold.

Cows milk: Keep milk in the coldest section of the refrigerator. Milk should be thrown out one week after its sell-by date.

Breast milk: Breast milk can be kept refrigerated for three to five days and frozen up to six month.

Formula milk: Ready-to-serve or concentrated formula can be refrigerated for up to 48 hours, while powered formula should be consumed within 24 hours.

Peanut butter: Adhere to expiration dates. Keep natural peanut butter in the refrigerator after opening. Regular peanut butter should be refrigerated after three months.

Pasta sauce: Tomato sauce is good for one week after opening.

Mayo-based salads: All mayo-based salads such as tuna, egg, chicken or macaroni should be thrown out after three to five days.

Salad greens: Most greens will last about five days.

Leftovers: Most leftovers can be safely consumed within three to four days; however, it is important to store them in several shallow containers rather than one deep container.

Source: ShopSmart August/September 2007 Issue

BATHROOMS

As the parent of multiples you will not be able to go the bathroom by yourself for several years. The master bath is full of dangerous, and messy stuff. The more you baby proof, the less stress you will have. In addition to locking the drawers and cabinets, you should secure the main entry to keep the babies in the room with you, instead of having them wandering through the house unattended.

Toilet locks are recommended for several reasons: to prevent drowning, the flushing of valuables, the plumbing bills that follow, and the "ick" factor of letting your child play in the toilet water. There are several toilet locks on the market. I recommend the Toilet lock from Kidco or the Lid Lock from Mommy's Helper.

Make sure your shower door does not open into the shower or you could end up with company from a toddler pushing on the door while you are inside.

Many master bathrooms have the closet in them as well. You will need to baby proof your closet by removing or securing strings, purse straps, belts, ties, etc. Remove plastic bags and any choking hazards. Some parents find it easier to just secure the closet door.

As the babies grow into a full-size tub, you will want to put on a tub faucet cover to prevent bumps and cuts. I recommend the Digital Spout Cover from 4Moms. This device is not only cushioned, but will give you a digital display of the water temperature as the tub is filling. Tub handles are excellent to aid the children in getting in and out of the tub. The Saf-er-Grip from Kidco is great for this purpose, and it is temporary as it is attached with heavy-duty suction cups.

PRODUCT PICKS

Tot Loks™ by Safety FirstBlindwinder™ from KidCo

Furniture wall straps from Safety First

Toilet lock from Kidco

Lid Lock from Mommy's Helper

Digital Spout Cover from 4Moms

Saf-er-Grip from Kidco

Crib Tent II™

NURSERY

In addition to the other items recommended, the nursery has a few different hazards. I recommend the Crib Tent II™ to keep the toddlers from climbing out of their crib. The Crib Tent II also keeps their arms and legs from getting stuck between the crib slats. You may use the crib tent up to 36-months, which is what I did and had zero issues with nap time and bedtime, as the children could not wander around.

Any toy box needs to have proper ventilation to prevent suffocation. If yours does not, simply drilling holes will solve the issue. I recommend not using a toy box at all.

Baby proofing your home will help to eliminate injuries. I recommend completely baby proofing the home prior to the baby crawling. The smartest parents baby proof their home prior to birth as this is one of the lowest stress points when starting a new family. This also gives the soon-to-be parents time to allow the use of their new baby proofing products to become second nature.

Every home is different, and not all hazards can be identified by simply reading a guide. The International Association For Child Safety (IAFCS) (www.iafcs.com) is a worldwide network of child safety professionals. IAFCS members are recognized baby proofing experts and are ready to help you make your home a safe place for your little ones.

All of the items discussed in this chapter are available at www.InfantHouse.com or by calling 1-866-infant5.

ADDITIONAL RESOURCES

- International Association For Child Safety- www. iafcs.com
- Safe Kids Worldwide- www.safekids.org
- American Academy of Pediatrics- www.aap.org
- International Association For Child Safety - http://69.13.128.173/findachildproofer.asp

FACTS ABOUT INJURIES TO CHILDREN AT HOME

In 2002, 5,305 children died from accidental injuries; approximately 40 percent of these deaths occurred in and around the home.

In 2003, approximately 1,900 children ages 14 and under died in the home from accidental injuries. Nearly 80 percent of these deaths occurred among children ages 4 and under.

Each year, there are an estimated 3.4 million visits to hospital emergency departments by children ages 14 and under for injuries that occurred in the home. Nearly 2 million of these visits are by children ages 4 and under.

Young children are at an increased risk from accidental injuries in the home because it is where they spend most of their time.

Accidental home injury deaths to children are caused primarily by airway obstruction, fire and burns, drowning, firearms, falls, choking and poisoning.

In 2003, an estimated 580 children ages 14 and under suffocated in the home. Of these children, nearly 90 percent were ages 4 and under.

In 2003, an estimated 350 children ages 14 and under died from fires and burns in the home. Nearly 60 percent were ages 4 and under.

In 2003, an estimated 320 children ages 14 and under drowned in or around the home. Of these children, more than 80 percent were ages 4 and under.

In 2003, an estimated 150 children ages 14 and under choked to death in the home. Of these children, nearly 90 percent were ages 4 and under.

In 2003, an estimated 60 children ages 14 and under died as the result of falls in the home. Of these children, nearly 70 percent were ages 4 and under.

In 2003, an estimated 50 children ages 14 and under died from poisonings in the home. Of these children, an estimated 60 percent were ages 4 and under.

In 2003, an estimated 40 children ages 14 and under died from unintentional shooting in the home. Of these children, half were ages 5 to 14.

Source: Safe Kids Worldwide®

Chapter 4

Easy Etiquette
Showers, Sip & Sees and Christenings

Babies bring with them an entire season of celebrations and social gatherings that are brand new to the mommy- and daddy-to-be. Knowing the ins-and-outs of social nuances associated with these occasions is as easy as it is essential.

SHOWER SHOULDS & SHOULD NOTS

Shower etiquette has evolved a great deal over the years. What was once considered to be gauche is now quite acceptable. For example, traditionally, it was considered inappropriate for a family member to host a shower. This was reserved for close friends, co-workers, and honorary aunts and godmothers-to-be. Now, it is quite acceptable to have a sister or cousin shower the mommy-to-be. The only people who should not host a shower are the grandmothers-to-be and the actual soon-to-be mommy herself.

While most showers for women carrying a singleton take place about two months prior to her delivery date, most women carrying multiples will not be up for anything social that far into gestation. As a matter of fact, you may very well already be a mommy. Women carrying multiples will begin their nesting much earlier, and therefore should have the shower no later than the fifth month of gestation. Ideally, you will still have time to wash and arrange all of your gifts and place them in their proper places throughout the house and nursery.

The southern tradition of gifting the hostess(es) of the shower with a Hostess Gift is not customary throughout the United States or throughout all cultures, but it is certainly a gesture that any hostess would appreciate. A hostess gift should be personal and specific to the hostess' personal style. Anything from fine chocolate and wine, to jewelry or flowers is an appropriate gift. The idea is to gift your hostess with something special to say, "thank you."

If it is impossible to have a shower prior to delivery due to medical complications, it is perfectly acceptable to have a Welcome Shower. However, plan to have the shower no sooner than one to two months after the babies have come home. You will need time to settle into your new life and your role as a mother before you are physically and emotionally ready to be social on such a grand scale.

Many women are blessed to have numerous friends and family members who would like to host a shower. While it is perfectly acceptable to have more than one shower, the same person should not host more than one.

Also, be conscientious of not inviting the same guests to multiple showers. While you may not expect them to purchase multiple gifts, they will feel obligated to so. Customarily, the hostess or hostesses cover the expense of the shower. This is their gift to the mommy-to-be and additional gifts should not be expected.

Register early in your pregnancy for your shower(s); many people will want to know in advance what your needs are and budget accordingly. Be sure to register at a location that is geographically and economically suitable for the majority of your guests. Many women have a standard gift they always bring for the mommy-to-be. While your registry is a list of items you need, it should not be considered an exclusive list of what to bring. So don't be offended if you receive many gifts that are not on your registry. These gifts may very well be the most treasured gifts of all. Utilize the Shower Registry Checklist when you go shopping for your registry.

SIP & SEES

The Sip & See is typically served at high tea time: 3:00 pm–5 pm. The hostess, who could be the mother or mother-in-law, a family member or friend, customarily serves finger foods, tea sandwiches, cookies and other small treats. Guests may bring small presents to the Sip & See; however, gifts are not the objective of the event as with a shower. Guests who bring gifts will most likely bring something that is considered more luxury then necessity. The purpose of a Sip & See is for the hostess to introduce friends and family to your new babies.

Much like a shower, the Sip & See is an occasion that should be offered by the hostess as a gift and not an expectation of the new mommy. This is a social occasion that should take place a couple of months post delivery. If someone offers to host a Sip & See in your honor, ask that they hold the event at least two months after the babies' homecoming. This will give you and your new little ones time to settle into your new life. And, much like a shower, your hostess will appreciate your thoughtfulness in providing a hostess gift.

CHRISTIAN & SECULAR CHRISTENINGS

The Christening is a ceremony that the new parents may choose to host. This is a special occasion that occurs in the first year of your babies' lives, or shortly thereafter, in which the parents dedicate their child (or in the case multiples— their children) in an intimate environment, amongst their closets friends and family to the faith, religion, or moral code in which they have chosen for their family. The guests should only include people who you believe will play an integral role in the spiritual development of your babies.

The parents typically provide a sit-down meal or buffet for the guests following the ceremony. Christening gifts given by your guests are generally silver, pewter or porcelain keepsakes such as a silver rattle or teething ring, a pewter cross, a silver loving cup or their first set of fine china.

The environment and dress should be elegantly casual. Your babies' may wear a Christening gown or some other heirloom garment. This is a spiritual occasion to be shared with your closest friends, family and spiritual mentors.

FORMS

- Baby Shower Gift Received & Thank You Form
- Sip & See Gift Received & Thank You Form
- Christening Gift Received & Thank You Form
- Registry Check list

Quick & Easy Hostess Gift Ideas

www.tylercandles.com
www.origins.com
www.arbonne.com
www.caldrea.com

ADDITIONAL RESOURCES

- Twinzgear.com offers unique and hard to find twins items for every member of the family. From shower gifts, nursing pillows, clothing, gifts for the family of twins, and even "Twingles" items for mothers of twins and a singleton, this store provides many of the must-have items. And, it is owned and operated by a family with twins, so they know what parents of multiples really need.

- Just4Twins.com is a great Web site for all things twins: cute t-shirts, onesies, ball caps, etc.

- Chat online with other moms-of-multiples at www.twinstuff.com.

- Tinyprints.com is a fantastic online store for custom invitation.

GIFT INFORMATION
& THANK YOU

CHAOS
2 CALM

Date	Description of Gift	From	Thank You Card Sent
04/09/2008	Bathroom Towels for Twins	Aunt Martha	Yes
04/11/2008	Carters Dresses and Blankets	Julie	Yes
04/12/2008	Flowers, Bottles and Burp Cloths	Jenny	No

BABY SHOWER THANK YOU

GIFT INFORMATION
& THANK YOU

Date	Description of Gift	From	Thank You Card Sent
06/09/2008	Piggy Bank for both Babies	Grandpa	No
06/09/2008	Diapers and wipes	Kristi	Yes
06/09/2008	Clothes from Carters 3-6 mo matching sets with matching blanket	Alicia	No

SIP & SEE THANK YOU

GIFT INFORMATION
& THANK YOU

CHRISTENING THANK YOU

Date	Description of Gift	From	Thank You Card Sent
09/01/2008	Frame with Cross for both babies, one pink, one purple with ducks	Kathleen & Trent	Yes
09/01/2008	Bracelet for both girls, names engraved on the inside	Great Grandma	Yes
09/01/2008	Shoes to go with gown, white with pink bows	Alicia	Yes

REGISTRY CHECKLIST

CHAOS 2 CALM

PERSONAL CARE

ITEM	QUANTITY PER BABY	RECEIVED	STILL NEED	GIVEN BY	THANK YOU NOTE SENT
Diapers	10/per baby/month	2 boxes		Kathy	no
Wipes	case		case	Grandma	yes
Diaper Rash Cream	2 tubes				
Mylicon	2 boxes	1	1	Kristi	yes
Breast Pump	1				
Pacifiers	4	4		Heather	yes
Pain Reliever Medicine	2 boxes				
First Aid Kit	1				
Humidifier	1				
Body Support Pillow	1				
milk storage bags	4 boxes				

KITCHEN

ITEM	QUANTITY PER BABY	RECEIVED	STILL NEED	GIVEN BY	THANK YOU NOTE SENT
Bottle	8				
Bottle Warmer	1				
Sterilizer	1				
Sippy Cups	3	3	3	Julie	yes
Flatware/Cutlery	3	3	3	Julie	yes
Plates/Bowls	3				
Bottle Drying Rack	1				
Bottle Brush	2				
Cabinet Locks	10				
Bibs	7	3			

CAR

ITEM	QUANTITY PER BABY	RECEIVED	STILL NEED	GIVEN BY	THANK YOU NOTE SENT
Infant Seat	1	2		Grandma	Yes
Toddler	1	2		Grandma	Yes
Roller Shade	1				
Car Mirror	1				
Seat Saver	1				

NURSERY

ITEM	QUANTITY PER BABY	RECEIVED	STILL NEED	GIVEN BY	THANK YOU NOTE SENT
Crib	1	2		Grandpa	Yes
Nursery Chair	just one				
Changing Table	1 up/1 downstairs				
Crib Sheets	2				
WATERPROOF MATTRESS PAD	2				
Clothing	8				
Sheet Protector	2				
Closet Size Organizer	1				
Hangers	20				
Blankets	2				
Chair Table	1 total				

BATHROOM

ITEM	QUANTITY PER BABY	RECEIVED	STILL NEED	GIVEN BY	THANK YOU NOTE SENT
Spout Cover	1 total				
Towels	3				
Wash Cloths	5				
Tub	1 total				
Tub Toys	3				
Shower Curtain	1 total				
Bath Mat	1 total				

TRAVEL

ITEM	QUANTITY PER BABY	RECEIVED	STILL NEED	GIVEN BY	THANK YOU NOTE SENT
Stroller	1 total	1		We bought	
Bjourn	2	1	1 total	We bought	
Diaper Bag	1 total				
Swaddler	2				
Pack and Play	1 total				

Chapter 5

Childcare Challenges

Whether you plan to work outside the home or not, you should seriously consider a full-or part-time nanny. Caring for multiple children can take its toll on even the most organized parents. Don't feel guilty employing help. You need time away from your children, and you will find that they will enjoy it as well. And, you and your spouse need to spend time together as a couple as often as possible, so as not to lose the "couple" at the head of the family. The occasional break from the children will actually help you be a better parent. We all need "me" time and that includes moms-of-multiples.

Begin lining up childcare as soon as you learn you are pregnant. If you live in a large urban area, you may be surprised to find that the childcare environment is quite competitive. It is not unusual to be on waiting lists for the entire duration of your pregnancy nor is it unusual to have to pay for childcare while you are still pregnant just to ensure the spots are reserved. If you will be returning to a professional career post-pregnancy, you will be grateful you did not procrastinate.

THE NANNY SEARCH

Finding the right nanny is as much an emotional decision as it is a financial decision. When looking for a nanny, start with your "mom" friends first. Ask your friends for advice and recommendations, inquire with other moms-of-multiples, check with women and bulletins at your church or synagogue, ask other moms at your OBGYN what their plans are and see if they have recommendations.

It is important to hire a professional—someone who truly cares and is knowledgeable about early child development. Caring for multiples is a highly demanding job; your nanny needs to have the qualifications necessary for success. Check with the Child Protective Service Agency in your state to find in-home nannies, as well as to check for any negative reports or complaints about a candidate you are considering hiring.

Simply put—be on the look out. Social recommendations are nice as they provide a built-in sense of trust, but be sure to follow up with thorough state and personal background checks and references.

Even if you come across several nannies through social recommendations that you like, do not neglect to contact several nanny services. Nanny services provide an additional layer of screening. They want to stay in business and enjoy repeat business and referrals just like any other company, so they have a stringent screening process for all their referrals. Again, don't just take the agencies' word for it, do your own research and call references.

HIRING NANNY

First and foremost, trust your gut. The most qualified person is not always the best. The best nanny for you may be a terrible choice for your neighbor. The top five considerations when interviewing a nanny are:

1. Qualifications: Does she have experience caring for multiples?
2. Reliable: Does she follow through with commitments?
3. Family Values: Are her core values in sync with yours? And if not, is she capable of supporting your core values with your children?
4. Common Discipline System: Does she subscribe to the same philosophy for discipline and is her threshold for discipline common to your own?
5. Pets: If you have pets, is she a natural animal lover or will your four-legged family members be neglected under her care?

SHE IS LIKE FAMILY

Your nanny will become like family; except, the nanny isn't family. It is imperative from the very beginning that these lines of familiarity are not crossed. The relationship between the nanny and parent is very unique. Nanny is a primary caregiver to your children and often grows to love them dearly. Your children will most likely reciprocate that affection and fondness. There is a very real possibility that your nanny will spend as much time, if not more, with your children as you. And this is exactly how the nanny becomes "like family."

The problem is that family does not call in sick, nor do they get paid. Family is not expected to vacuum the carpet, mop the floor, tend to laundry or make the beds, all of which are not unusual jobs for the nanny. So really, as wonderful as the nanny is, she is not like family. She is an employee, and it is important to treat her as such to prevent complications within this unique relationship.

THE NANNY EMPLOYEE HANDBOOK

Create a Nanny Employee Handbook. This book will assist your nanny, but it is ultimately a record keeping system for you. Purchase a three-ring binder with dividers, and create the following labels for your dividers:

PART 1 - THE NANNY BOOK

- Emergency Numbers: Parents' cell phone and office, closest relative, neighbors, close friend, non-emergency police department, non-emergency fire department, poison control and 911.

- Allergy and other medical information: Also have an updated Allergy and Medical Information form for each child included in the nanny book. While this may seem litigious, it is important that you do not allow the nanny to administer any medication without your written request. Use the Medication Administration form included on the CD to keep track of your babies' medicinal intake in your absence.

- Baby Feeding & Activity Schedule: Each day, have your nanny keep track of your babies' feeding (how much they eat and at what time) and bowel movements with the Feeding & Activity Schedule. These records will help you stay connected to your babies' day-to-day experiences and will be very helpful in making dietary adjustments as your babies grow and develop.

- To-Do List: The Daily To-Do List will help you assign duties to your nanny for each day of the week. From laundry to tumbling classes, this daily form is your nanny's little book of instructions.

- Notes: The notes section is where you and your nanny communicate on the days where you may not actually see one another or where small comments can be noted from either one of you. This section ensures effective communication between the two of you.

PART II - EMPLOYEE HANDBOOK

The best relationships are those in which boundaries are well established in writing. Protect your relationship with your nanny by treating her like an employee.

- Job Description: Provide a detailed description and expectations of your nanny's jobs. What are her primary, secondary and tertiary responsibilities? Be specific and detailed.

- Employee Policies: Prior to your nanny's first day, have a written employee policy.

- How personal time off (sick/ vacation days) will be handled?

- What is the "call-in" policy if your nanny will not be able to make it?

- What is your policy about the nanny's children coming to work with her?

- What is the transportation policy?

- What is the phone policy?

The Nanny Book is your nanny's guide to caring for your child. You can find sample forms for the Nanny Book at the end of this chapter, as well as blank forms on the accompanying disk.

FAMILY ORIENTATION

Provide your nanny with an orientation to your family prior to her first day on the job. Tour the home and go over the small nuances of the house that she will want to "look out for." Explain your typical routine, (see sample Activity Schedule form).

Discuss with your nanny your family's core values. Her support and understanding of these values are essential to instilling them in your children. Share with your nanny your religious beliefs to avoid confusing or conflicting messages. Use the TV Policy form to enforce TV rules while your nanny is caring for the children. Create a Pool Policy form. Laminate it and post it in clear view when pool side, etc.

DAYCARE

You may find that your needs are better served in a daycare center. Daycare has become a highly competitive industry. You will find some day cares provide very elaborate services and are more focused towards fun and entertainment, while others are educationally focused.

When shopping for a daycare, consider your five-year plan. If you know you want your child in a specific school at two years of age, such as in Montessori or Waldorf School, you only need to evaluate the actual infant classrooms. If you intend to have your child remain in daycare until Kindergarten, then you will need to be very thorough in your daycare selection.

Shopping for daycare can be a truly challenging experience. You may experience guilt, sadness and worry about being separated from your babies. You may fear that your babies will be highly stressed or emotionally scarred by being separated from you every day. However, you will find that in the right environment, daycare can actually play a very positive role in your babies' early development. Language skills, potty training and social skills are all impacted by

> You will find some day cares provide very elaborate services and are more focused towards fun and entertainment, while others are educationally focused.

exterior influences. In a clean, safe, and calm environment, your children will truly benefit from socializing with their classmates, as well as other adults.

STEPS TO CHOOSING A DAYCARE

1. Start with asking your pediatrician, friends and family for daycare recommendations. Use the Daycare Shopping Guide to assist in this process.

2. Search the Internet for Child Protective Services for your state. This state agency will log all reports of state regulatory non-compliance for every licensed daycare center, as well as licensed home care providers. Use the Daycare Shopping Guide to list the daycare centers and contact information for each daycare you are interested in touring.

3. Call ahead to schedule a tour of the daycare. Do not drop by unannounced on your first visit. Some centers only provide tours on specific days and times. While some centers will tour "drop-ins," you do not want to be rushed through the tour or be asked to wait for a long period while the administrator finishes her task at hand. You will have a much better experience.

4. After touring all of the centers on your list, narrow your selection to the top three in which you are most interested. Use the Top Three Daycare Shopping Guide for your second visit. The second visit is when you "drop-in" without notice. Let the administrator know that you do not need to occupy her time but simply that you would like to observe one or several of the classrooms quietly for 30 minutes. Make notes on your form to review later.

5. Make your decision and pay your deposit!

FORMS

- Caregiver Application
- Caregiver Agreement Form
- Employee Policy
- Caregiver Job Description
- Daily To-Do List
- Emergency Contact Numbers
- Medication Administration
- Allergy & Other Medical Information
- TV Policy
- Pool Policy
- Activity Schedule
- Daycare Shopping Guide
- Top Three Day cares
- Communication Log

ADDITIONAL RESOURCE

- Care.com is a great Web site for parents seeking in-home nanny care. Just type in your zip code and start searching for caregivers in your area. www.care.com

APPLICANT INFORMATION

Name	*Mrs. Jane Lee*
Address	*1234 Memory Lane*
City	*Plano*
State	*TX*
Zip Code	*75024*
Phone Number	*972-555-5555*
Fax Number	
Email	*any@any.com*

Education

High School	*ABC High School*	College	*ABC College*
Address	*1234 School Road*	Address	*1234 School Rd*
Did you graduate?	*Yes*	Did you graduate?	*Yes*
Date	*01/01/01*	Date	*01/01/01*
Degree	*General*	Degree	*Childhood Edu*
Email	*any@any.com*	Email	*any@any.com*

Additional Education

Took CPR classes at local hospital.

Special Skills

Love being with children and teaching about the world.

Previous Employment

Name of Employer	*Starbucks*	Dates of Employment	*01/01/08*
Reason for leaving	*Still Employed*	Position	*Customer Service*

Duties/Responsibilities *Cashier, make coffee, clean up at closing, counting money, restocking.*

Name of Employer		Dates of Employment	
Reason for leaving		Position	

Duties/Responsibilities

Name of Employer		Dates of Employment	
Reason for leaving		Position	

Duties/Responsibilities

CAREGIVER APPLICATION

CHAOS 2 CALM

Name	Mary Jo	Name	
Address	1234 Any Road	Address	
City	Dallas	City	
State	TX	State	
Zip Code	75225	Zip Code	
Phone Number	972-555-5555	Phone Number	
Relationship	Friend	Relationship	
Years of Acquaintance	5	Years of Acquaintance	

Name	Sally Sue	Name	
Address	1234 Any Road	Address	
City	Phoenix	City	
State	AZ	State	
Zip Code	85023	Zip Code	
Phone Number	972-555-5555	Phone Number	
Relationship	Friend	Relationship	
Years of Acquaintance	10	Years of Acquaintance	

Name		Name	
Address		Address	
City		City	
State		State	
Zip Code		Zip Code	
Phone Number		Phone Number	
Relationship		Relationship	
Years of Acquaintance		Years of Acquaintance	

By signing below, you agree that all of the information in this application is true to the full extent of your knowledge.

_____   _____

Applicant   Date

Customer Information

Name	**Sally Jo**
Address	**1234 Hall St.**
City	**Dallas**
State	**TX**
Zip Code	**75225**
Phone Number	**972-555-5555**
Fax Number	
Email	**sally@email.com**

Child Care Provider Information

Name	**Melissa Smith**
Address	**1234 Hall Ave.**
City	**Dallas**
State	**TX**
Zip Code	**75225**
Phone Number	**972-555-1234**
Fax Number	
Email	

Children's Information

Name	**Peyton Alexis**	Name	**Sydney Morgan**
Birth Date	**04/07/2007**	Birth Date	**04/07/2007**
Name		Name	
Birth Date		Birth Date	

special notes:

Description of services to be provided:

The Customer hereby agrees to engage Child Care Provider to provide the Customer with the following services:

Light household duties including: making master bedroom bed, washing and putting dishes away, making children's beds, taking the trash out and laundry.

Duties and tasks both parties agree on as outlined below:

As needed to take the trash to the curb on trash day.

Terms of Agreement

This agreement becomes effective on the following date: __01/01/2009__
and will remain in effect until either party provides a fourteen day written notice of termination or resignation.

CAREGIVER AGREEMENT FORM

CHAOS 2 CALM

Hourly

Weekly

Monthly   **$1500.00**

Fixed Rate

Per Child Rate

Additional Compensation

$500.00 Christmas Bonus and 1 week paid vacation upon completion

and execution of the agreement.

Child Care Provider Confidence Agreement

By signing this document the Child Care Provider agrees to hold in confidence all of

Customer's personal family matters including:

Bank account information, medical files, credit card information given,

social security numbers and computer files.

Customer	Date

Child Care Provider	Date

Disclaimer:
The intent of this form is to provide information in regard to the subject matter covered. This form is purchased with the understanding that the publisher and author and advisors are not rendering legal, accounting, medical or any other professional services. The author, advisors and publisher shall have neither liability nor responsibility to any person or entity with respect to any loss or damage caused or alleged to be caused directly or indirectly by the information contained in this form.

CAREGIVER AGREEMENT FORM

CHAOS 2 CALM

Child Care Provider Hours

Monday	**8-5**
Tuesday	
Wednesday	**8-5**
Thursday	
Friday	**8-5**
Saturday	***Every other Saturday 6pm - 10pm. Date nights.***
Sunday	

Sick Day Policy
List the number of sick days allowed per calendar year. Indicate whether or not these days are paid or unpaid. Indicate whether not these days rollover to the following calendar year. Note the call-in policy for utilizing sick days.

4 sick days allowed per calendar year (unpaid).

Personal Day Policy
List the number of personal days allowed per calendar year. Indicate whether or not these days are paid or unpaid. Indicate whether not these days rollover to the following calendar year. Note the call-in policy for utilizing personal days.

5 personal days per year (paid).

Tardy or No-Show Policy
Indicate your policy regarding tardiness or "no-showing."
How will these situations be dealt with.

No-Shows are not accepted.

Policy Regarding Bringing Children To Work
May your child care provider bring his or her own children to work? If, so, what are the stipulations regarding this policy?

Not allowed unless presented on special circumstances.

For example, if your child is out of school for the day and

they are not an interruption to the household.

Additional

Child Care Provider Job Description

Hours Responsibilities Shall Be Performed

Monday	**8-5**
Tuesday	
Wednesday	**8-5**
Thursday	
Friday	**8-5**
Saturday	
Sunday	

Primary Responsibilities

Provide the best beneficial care for the twins. Adhere to the schedule as close as possible and use the communication sheet that is provided to the best of your ability. Perform household duties that are ex-plained above. Provide any ideas or suggestions to help with the care of the twins. Teach and love our children to the best of your ability.

Secondary Responsibilities

Tertiary Responsibilities

Additional Responsibilities

CHILD CARE PROVIDER DAILY TO-DO LIST

7:00 am	Follow Feeding Schedule for the babies as close as you can.
7:30 am	
8:00 am	
8:30 am	
9:00 am	Laundry
9:30 am	Dishes
10:00 am	Wash Bottles
10:30 am	Make Bottles
11:00 am	
11:30 am	
12:00 pm	
12:30 pm	
1:00 pm	
1:30 pm	
2:00 pm	
2:30 pm	
3:00 pm	
3:30 pm	
4:00 pm	
4:30 pm	
5:00 pm	Get dinner ready for babies first, then mom and dad.
5:30 pm	
6:00 pm	
6:30 pm	
7:00 pm	

Emergency **911**	Poison Control
Non-Emergency	Non-Emergency
Fire Department **972-555-5555**	Police Department

Home Address	
Address	
City	
State	
Zip Code	
Phone Number	

Mom Full Name	**Mamma Mia**	Dad Full Name	**Papa Mia**
Cell Phone	**214-555-5555**	Cell Phone	**214-555-5555**
Business Phone	**972-555-5555**	Business Phone	**972-555-5555**
Email	**any@any.com**	Email	**any@any.com**
Other		Other	

Pediatrician	**Dr. Any**	Emergency Pediatrician	**Dr. Any**
Address	**1234 Memory Road**	Address	**1234 Memory Road**
City	**Dallas**	City	**Dallas**
State	**TX**	State	**TX**
Zip Code	**75225**	Zip Code	**75225**
Phone Number	**972-555-5555**	Phone Number	**972-555-5555**

Veterinarian		Emergency Veterinarian	
Address		Address	
City		City	
State		State	
Zip Code		Zip Code	
Phone Number		Phone Number	

Grandparent 1	**Grandma A**	Grandparent 2	**Grandma B**
Address	**1234 Any Road**	Address	**1234 Any Road**
City	**Albuquerque**	City	**Dallas**
State	**NM**	State	**TX**
Zip Code	**87111**	Zip Code	**75234**
Phone Number	**505-555-5555**	Phone Number	**972-555-5555**
Cell Phone		Cell Phone	

EMERGENCY CONTACT NUMBERS

Grandparent 3	Grandparent 4
Address	Address
City	City
State	State
Zip Code	Zip Code
Phone Number	Phone Number
Cell Phone	Cell Phone

Neighbor 1 *Mr. and Mrs. Smith*	Neighbor 2 *Mr. and Mrs. Smith*
Address *1234 Any Road*	Address *1234 Any Road*
City *Dallas*	City *Dallas*
State *TX*	State *TX*
Zip Code *75023*	Zip Code *75023*
Phone Number *972-555-5555*	Phone Number *972-555-5555*
Cell Phone	Cell Phone

Neighbor 3	Neighbor 4
Address	Address
City	City
State	State
Zip Code	Zip Code
Phone Number	Phone Number
Cell Phone	Cell Phone

School 1 *Any School*	School 2
Address *1234 Any Road*	Address
City *Dallas*	City
State *TX*	State
Zip Code *75023*	Zip Code
Phone Number *972-555-5555*	Phone Number
Teacher Number *972-555-5555*	Teacher Number

Other Contact 1	Other Contact 2
Address	Address
City	City
State	State
Zip Code	Zip Code
Phone Number	Phone Number
Cell Phone	Cell Phone

MEDICATION ADMINISTRATION FORM

1. Medication shall only be administered by ***parent unless authorized***
(name of child care provider) under the direction of a Medical Administration Form.

2. Medication will always be in its original, childproof container.

3. Medication must always be stored out of the reach of all children.

Prescription Medication
Medication shall be administered in accordance with the pharmacy label directions as prescribed by the child's health care provider.

Non-Prescription (Over-the-Counter) Medications
1. May be administered only under the direction of parent and must be accompanied with a signed Medical Administration Form.

2. Non-prescription medication shall be administered in accordance with the product label directions on the container.

Authorization for Medication Administration
I hereby authorize (name of authorized agent): _____
to administer the following medication to my child (name of child)   ***Peyton & Sydney***_____

Parent/Guardian Name	**Mr. and Mrs. Smith**
Phone Number	**972-555-5555**
Health Care Provider	**ABC Pediatrics**
Phone Number	**972-555-5555**
Purpose of Medication is	**Reflux**

Time of Administration: **9:00 am**
Time of Administration:
Time of Administration:
Time of Administration:

Name of Medication:
Method of Administration:
Possible Side Effects:
In case of an emergency contact: **ABC Pediatrics or dial 911**
Phone Number: **972-555-5555**

Parent/Guardian Signature
Today's Date:

ALLERGY & OTHER MEDICAL INFORMATION

Name *Peyton Alexis*

Blood Type *O+*

Social Security Number *555-55-5555*

Medicinal Allergies

Food Allergies

Medical Conditions

Allergy & Other Medical Information

Name *Sydney Morgan*

Blood Type *O+*

Social Security Number *555-55-5555*

Medicinal Allergies

Food Allergies

Medical Conditions

Disclaimer:
The intent of this form is to provide information in regard to the subject matter covered. This form is purchased with the understanding that the publisher and author and advisors are not rendering legal, accounting, medical or any other professional services. The author, advisors and publisher shall have neither liability nor responsibility to any person or entity with respect to any loss or damage caused or alleged to be caused directly or indirectly by the information contained in this form.

TELEVISION & MOVIE POLICY

List of networks children are allowed to view.

None at this time, maybe when they get a little older.

List of shows children are allowed to view.

Baby Einstein once a day.

List of shows/movies/networks children are never allowed to view.

None at this time.

Number of hours per day children may view television.

None at this time.

Particular times children are allowed to view television.

7:00 am	1:30 pm
7:30 am	2:00 pm
8:00 am	2:30 pm
8:30 am	3:00 pm
9:00 am *Baby Einstein*	3:30 pm
9:30 am	4:00 pm
10:00 am	4:30 pm
10:30 am	5:00 pm
11:00 am	5:30 pm
11:30 am	6:00 pm
12:00 pm	6:30 pm
12:30 pm	7:00 pm
1:00 pm	7:30 pm

POOL POLICY

Pool Supervision Policy. Indicate your policy regarding supervision.

At this time we are electing to NOT have the children in the pool. This may be changed or

updated at a later time.

Friends Swimming Policy. Indicate your policy regarding having friends over for swimming (nanny's and children's).

Due to the many accidents in pools, no one will be allowed to use the pool

unless the parents are home.

Pool Snacks & Refreshments Policy. Indicate your policy regarding food and beverages near pool (nanny's and children's).

No food outside, only bottled water.

Pool Alarm Codes

1234#

Number of hours per day children may swim per day.

Particular times children are allowed to swim.

7:00 am	1:30 pm
7:30 am	2:00 pm
8:00 am	2:30 pm
8:30 am	3:00 pm
9:00 am	3:30 pm
9:30 am	4:00 pm
10:00 am	4:30 pm
10:30 am	5:00 pm
11:00 am	5:30 pm
11:30 am	6:00 pm
12:00 pm	6:30 pm
12:30 pm	7:00 pm
1:00 pm	7:30 pm

ACTIVITY SCHEDULE

7:00 am

7:30 am

8:00 am

8:30 am

9:00 am

9:30 am

10:00 am

10:30 am

11:00 am

11:30 am

12:00 pm

12:30 pm

1:00 pm

1:30 pm

2:00 pm

2:30 pm

3:00 pm

3:30 pm

4:00 pm

4:30 pm

5:00 pm

5:30 pm

6:00 pm

6:30 pm

7:00 pm

DAYCARE SHOPPING GUIDE

Daycare Shopping Guide

1. Compile a list of daycare centers based on referrals you have received from your pediatrician, friends, family and personal research.

2. Search the Internet for Child Protective Services for your state. This state agency will log all reports of state regulatory non-compliance for every licensed daycare center, as well as licensed home care providers. Make notes about the facilities that interest you. Please note, it is rare for facility to receive a perfect score at every state agency observation. Do not eliminate a facility based on a few of non-compliances; however you should do additional research to determine the severity of the non-compliance and the circumstances surrounding the non-compliance.

3. Call to schedule a tour of the daycare. Do not drop by unannounced on your first visit. Some centers only provide tours on specific days and times. While some centers will tour "drop-ins," you do not want to be rushed through the tour or be asked to wait for a long period while the administrator finishes his or her task at hand. Remember, she has a job to do outside of being the center tour guide. Be polite and call ahead. You will have a much better experience.

4. Notes:

    Called ABC Daycare, responded quickly. Kathy called me back, seemed friendly and was

    very interested in setting up an appointment with our family.

DAYCARE SHOPPING GUIDE

Rank this facility from 1 to 10 with 10 being the highest ranking:

Facility Name **ABC Daycare**

Address **1234 Hall St.**

Phone Number **972-555-5555**

Web site **www.abcdaycare.com**

Tour Date **01/01/08**

Tour Notes **Felt very comfortable with the teachers. ALL of the kids were playing**

and interacting with each other. The room looked clean and organized.

We were impressed with the overall setting.

Rank this facility from 1 to 10 with 10 being the highest ranking:

Facility Name **DFG Daycare**

Address **123 Any Street**

Phone Number **972-555-5555**

Web site **www.dfgdaycare.com**

Tour Date **01/02/08**

Tour Notes **The rooms were very nice, but the kids must have been having a bad**

day. They didn't seem to be interacting with the teachers. The visit was

rushed, and I felt like I was pushed out the door.

Rank this facility from 1 to 10 with 10 being the highest ranking:

Facility Name

Address

Phone Number

Web site

Tour Date

Tour Notes

After touring all of the centers on your Daycare Shopping Guide, use your ranking system to narrow your selections to the top three.

The second visit is when you "drop-in" without notice. Let the administrator know that you do not need to occupy her time but simply that you would like to observe one or several of the classrooms quietly for 30 minutes. Make notes on your form to review later.

During your observation note the following:

Facility Name:	**ABC Daycare**
Administrator Name:	**Sally Jo**
Phone Number:	**972-555-5555**

1. How many teachers are in the classroom you observed? Is the classroom within the state required student to teacher ratio (you can find this information on your local child protective services Web site)?

    2 teachers were in the classroom. There were only eight students and seemed like a very nice class our children would love.

2. Are the teachers courteous to the children?

    Yes, they were so excited to see the twins. Both teachers wanted to scoop the babies up and take them in today!

3. Are the teachers talking with the children or with each other?

    Yes, constant communication especially with the toddlers.

4. Do the children seem happy? Are they clean?

    Yes, children seem to have fun and were exceptionally clean.

5. Is the classroom organized and clean?

    The classroom was very organized and kept clean considering they have eight children.

6. Does the room smell nice or like a diaper pail?

Smells nice, but you could tell a few diapers had been changed.

7. Is the classroom structured to be child-friendly, or teacher-friendly?

Both, which I think is important.

8. Are the teachers uncomfortable with your presence?

NO. Both teachers were very happy to answer questions

and show us around with out any problems.

Additional notes and observations:

ABC Daycare is the place for us!

On a scale of one to ten, how do you rank this facility based on your second observation?

10

COMMUNICATION LOG

Date:

From Parent:

Peyton seems to be very happy today and Sydney is a bit sleepy. Please try to keep up with the tummy time and burp them both really good so we can control the gas.

Date:

From Child Care Provider:

Peyton was very attentive today. Slept really well during the first nap, the second nap was short. Sydney did great. She was a bit sleepy, but did great when I woke her up. Had to give .3 of Mylicon to control the gas. Great little babies.

Chapter 6

Nest & Rest

*Whether domesticity is a chore or a joy in your life, you will
innately become a domestic diva throughout your pregnancy and
certainly in your last months. Most women start feeling the urge
to nest in their fifth month, and some women even experience
an acute need for nesting in the hours before labor. The nesting
instinct is the distinctive urge to clean, tidy and organize your
home and life in preparation for your babies-to-be. While the
urge to nest is greatest in your last months, moms-of-multiples
need to get their nesting out of their system earlier than most, as
they will most likely not carry to full term.*

If you are an extreme nester be sure to play it safe, and let someone else do the tough tasks.
Be sure to take frequent breaks and stay rested. Moms-to-be should definitely delegate the
following tasks:

NESTING NO-NOS

1. *Paint.* Painting is laborious work, and balancing on a ladder with a big belly is just
   not a good idea! Also, many paints contain toxic substances that are not good for
   anyone, especially a pregnant woman.

2. *Kitty Litter.* Take a nine-month break from being the designated kitty pooper-
   scooper. Indoor/outdoor cats run the risk of infection by a parasite called
   toxoplasmosis. This parasite can be transferred through fecal matter and can
   cause severe health complications and birth defects to unborn babies.

3. *Certain Household Cleaners.* If you have wanted to hire a housekeeper and have not
   yet employed one, now is a great time to do it. It is also prudent to replace all your
   conventional household cleaners with non-toxic, all-natural cleaners. If you must
   clean, avoid oven cleaners and dry cleaning products. Avoid any ammonia/chlorine
   combinations and wear protective gloves.

Nesting is a wonderful aspect of pregnancy. Take advantage of your nesting instinct to really get your home in tip-top shape and ready for the babies. This is also a good time pack your hospital bag. You will only need the bare necessities as the hospital provides just about everything you will need.

MOM'S HOSPITAL BAG

- Comfortable clothing for the journey home
- Your favorite pillow if you have one
- Socks
- Two sets of warm sleepwear
- Two nursing bras
- Basic toiletries
- Cord-Blood Registry kit

PARTNER'S HOSPITAL BAG

- Basic Toiletries
- Digital camera
- Video camera
- Back massager and massage lotions or oils for labor
- Phone charger
- Call list

BABIES' HOMECOMING BAG

- Layettes, hats and booties for each baby
- Two receiving blankets for each baby
- Fully stocked diaper bag
- Car seat for each baby

REST & READINESS

The urge to nest peaks in the fifth month, just around the time that moms-of-multiples-to-be should be getting the most rest. While the urge to nest may be great, be careful not to overdo it.

Spend plenty of time in bed, relaxing on the sofa or

lounging on the chaise lounge outside. This is the last time you will have so much down time for decades; enjoy it while you can.

Listen to soothing music and take your time writing thank you notes for your shower gifts and the many thoughtful gestures your friends have most likely demonstrated. Search the Internet for baby announcements. Go ahead and order your announcements now so you can address the envelopes and be ready to send them out as soon as you come home with the babies.

Spend time with your journal every day during this time. Journaling will help you to explore your feelings and emotions about your pregnancy, as well as your pending new role as a mom-of-multiples. You will probably enjoy sharing this journal with your children some day.

BED REST (LESS·NESS)

From the moment a woman learns she is pregnant, her protective instincts kick in. Knowing that your babies are in distress and the only thing you can personally do is lie flat on your back for weeks on end to help them creates a sense of tremendous powerlessness and fear.

During this time, follow your doctors' advice and get as comfortable as you can. And, know there actually are some things you can start doing now to prepare for your babies' arrival. Using this time to prepare will not only help you pass the time, but will also give your restless mind some much needed focus.

SURVIVING BED REST IN THE HOSPITAL

If your doctor prescribes in-patient bed rest, be prepared for dealing with solitude. While your partner, family and friends will provide support, the fact is they all have a life that must be tended to on a daily basis. The following tips will help you survive the monotony of daily life in a hospital bed.

- If you do not already own one, send your honey to the store for a portable DVD player.

- Develop a meal schedule with your family

and friends. Hospital food is nutritious not delicious. You can also make special orders from the cafeteria if someone is not bringing you food from outside the hospital.

- Make your hospital bed your own. Bring your comforter, body pillow, egg crate, etc. You need to create a space that is as comfortable and personal as possible.

Good to Know

If you find yourself on any type of bed rest, you will need to be conscious of exercising your legs to keep the blood circulating and prevent blood clots. Because every woman who experiences bed rest is different, be sure to ask your doctor the following questions regarding your specific condition, and follow his or her advice without exception:

- May I get up to walk to the bathroom?
- May I get up to prepare meals or to do light chores?
- May I take a bath or shower, and if so, which is preferable?
- What is the best position to be in while resting?
- Is it okay for me to work from home?
- Is driving safe?
- How much walking is safe?
- How much and what kind of sexual activity is safe?
- What activities can I safely do to increase blood circulation?

- Put friends and family on reading rotation so you always have up-to-date magazines and current novels to read.

- Bring your laptop. You can shop, do research and even pay bills if you need to. Stay connected to friends and family versus continuously updating everyone by phone.

- Don't feel obligated to take calls. Turn the ringer off if you need privacy. This is your time.

- Let your nurse know what times of the day you need privacy and have a sign placed on your door to knock before entering. You may not want your boss, who is kindly making a visit, to see you when you are not expecting it.

- Bring a small refrigerator so you can have your own snacks and drinks at hand.

- If you enjoy knitting, cross-stitching, scrapbooking, etc., this is a great way to productively pass the time.

- Schedule at least one visitor a day!

AT-HOME BED REST

If your doctor prescribes at-home bed rest, you may feel lucky that you are not trapped in the hospital. In many ways, it is wonderful to be in the comfort of your own home, but it certainly has its challenges. Because many times the mom-to-be feels fine, the temptation to get out of bed and do easy work around the house can be torturous. Don't do it!

At-home bed rest can also be more isolating than hospital care. At the hospital, you have all the help you need 24/7, while at home you will have to wait for someone to help you. Your partner may be at work and your friends and family won't always be there.

The following tips will help you stay productive and help you pass the time.

- Create a self-contained space:
    1. Have a make-up station next to your bed (you feel better when you look better).
    2. Create a workstation next to the bed with your phone, fax and laptop.
    3. Have your husband, partner, friend or family member make you breakfast, lunch, snacks and beverages each day, and put it in a cooler next to your bed.
    4. Create an entertainment area: books, magazines, a portable DVD player that you do not have to get up to access, etc.
- Don't feel guilty sleeping. Get as much rest as possible!
- If you do not have a housekeeper, hire one. If that is not a possibility, ask a friend to coordinate a group of friends to rotate cleaning for you. It is hard to ask people to help but your friends want to and will gladly do so. Their assistance is a gift. Accept it.
- Write personal thank you letters rather than emails.
- Have a daily routine. This will help you pace the days and keep a healthy attitude about your situation.

ADDITIONAL RESOURCES
- KnockKnock.biz sells fun and creative Thank You cards.
- Join the blogging community on BabyCenter.com.

Chapter 7

Homecoming
Getting Settled into a New Way of Life

Once you bring your babies home from the hospital, life as you know it will never be the same. These precious bundles of joy will keep you on your toes for the next twenty years. But first, you have to survive the first twenty days!

Prepare ahead of time for help. You will need physical, emotional and interpersonal coping strategies. Use the Sign Up To Assist form, and ask your friends and family to volunteer for a couple of hours at a time. It is very common for multiples to be born pre-maturely, in which case they often spend some time in the Neo-Natal Intensive Care Unit (NICU). Your babies may not be discharged from the hospital at the same as you, and one baby will likely be discharged before the other. You will need physical support in order to spend time with your babies. And, you will need emotional support to get you through this life changing time.

It is absolutely essential that you are able to take care of yourself physically. As hard as it is to sleep when you have multiple babies, you will be able to provide for them better if you are rested. Friends and family will generously provide meals; don't turn them down. If someone offers to help, accept the help. You will learn very quickly that you cannot do everything yourself.

Postpartum sadness or depression is normal and is nothing to be ashamed or embarrassed of. Your body undergoes tremendous change during pregnancy and delivery, and it is not uncommon to be emotionally stressed. Set realistic goals for yourself. Be open with your feelings, and allow yourself to discuss your fears about your new journey ahead. Continue journaling. Journaling is a very powerful exercise for emotional release. Allow yourself to be assertive and express your needs openly.

Focus on your interpersonal needs as well. Communicate with your spouse and family members. Be conscious that everyone is going through an equally exciting and stressful time. Create time just for you and your spouse with your new babies. While friends and family mean well by dropping by, let your visitors know that you need scheduled visits in order to keep your babies routine stable and for you to heal.

If you have singleton children already, remember to be sensitive to their feelings about how the arrival of the new babies may impact their perception of their role in the family. Be careful to not delegate tasks to your additional children. While it may be easy to utilize them as helpers, keep in mind they had no say in the arrival of these new babies. Your singleton children may need some time to adjust before they are ready to embrace the idea of assisting in their siblings' care.

Include your singleton children in pregnancy by taking them with you to see the babies during the sonograms. Share the sonogram pictures with your singletons and talk about the growth and development of the babies throughout the pregnancy.

TIPS FOR PREPARING YOUR SINGLETONS FOR MULTIPLES

1. Include your older children in the process of preparing for the arrival of the new babies by allowing them to pick out clothing and décor items for the nursery.

2. If you are given a shower, allow your older children to assist in opening the presents and creating thank you cards.

3. Go through your older children's baby books with them and reminisce with them about their own homecoming experience.

4. When possible make adjustments to your children's schedules prior to the multiples coming home to minimize the shift in their own routines.

5. Allow your singleton children to select a "big sister" or "big brother" gift for each of the babies. Purchase or make a gift for each of your singleton children to be given by the babies.

6. When you pack your own bag for the hospital, pack a bag for your singleton child as well and include art supplies, books, snacks, a Big Brother or Big Sister t-shirt and his or her own disposable camera.

7. Make arrangements for in-home care for your children so they are not removed from their home environment while you are in the hospital.

8. If possible, say goodbye to your singleton child or children, and call home frequently from the hospital.

9. When your child visits you in the hospital, allow him or her to hold the babies (under supervision). When your child is finished holding the babies, pass them to another adult or nurse and snuggle with your singleton child.

10. Spend private time with your older children when you come home from the hospital. Include them in time with the babies, but also create individual time.

11. When others make a big "to-do" about the babies, be sure to bring your older child into the conversation by commenting on what a help she has been.

BREASTFEEDING YOUR BABIES

Premature babies often are not yet strong enough to nurse from the breast. You can initiate the mommy-to-baby bond that develops as a result of breastfeeding by using the Kangaroo Care technique. Kangaroo Care is a term used to describe a method of care for all newborns, but in particular for premature babies, with the following three components:

1. Skin-to-skin contact
2. Exclusive breastfeeding
3. Support to the mother infant dyad.

Skin-to-skin is specifically the contact between the baby's front and the mother's bare chest. This allows the baby to have a full sensorial experience with the mother through touch, smell, vision and hearing her voice. This contact will be a catalyst for the mother's milk flow.

Exclusive breastfeeding means that the baby only

Good to Know

The Advantages of Breastfeeding Premature Multiples

- Human breast milk is easier to digest and better tolerated by most premature infants than formula. Proteins in human milk, unlike proteins in formulas, are completely broken down and absorbed by the human digestive system.
- The enzyme lipase, which is contained in breast milk, helps babies digest milk fat more efficiently. Fat is an important source of energy for premature babies' growth.
- Human milk contains extra defenses against infection. Antibodies give a premature baby's immature immune system protection from potentially serious bacterial and viral infections.
- Research suggests that human milk contains hormones and enzymes, including certain growth factors important to your babies' maturity, digestive and nervous systems.

continued...

receives milk from the mother either through direct suckling or via expressing. However, premature babies often need additional supplements in order to obtain proper nutrition.

Support to the dyad means that whatever is needed for the medical, emotional, psychological and physical well being of mother and baby is provided to them, without separating them. Once again, premature babies may have to be separated from the mother for periods of time if they are in the NICU.

Breastfeeding multiples is truly a full-time job that requires a great deal of organization. Common problems such as sore or cracked nipples, engorgement, low milk supply and concern as to how much milk each baby is actually getting can all seem overwhelming. Enlist the support of your baby's doctor, lactation specialist and other moms-of-multiples, and you will find multi-tasking skills you never knew you had!

Breastfeeding and bottle-feeding take about the same amount time with regard to the actual feeding. However, preparing formula bottles, shopping for formula and warming bottles all take a significant amount of time.

If you are able and have the desire to breastfeed, you will find that your body will naturally keep you on a feeding/pumping schedule. Because each child consumes varying amounts, it is good to alternate breasts with each baby so as to keep your breasts producing equally and to reduce the risk of developing a blocked milk duct.

A nursing pillow designed for multiples is very effective and can free your hands to burp one baby in rotation. There will be times when only one child is breastfeeding this is a great time to keep up the multi-tasking by pumping the other breast.

You will want to keep a couple of bottles of water at each of your nursing stations. The body releases oxytocin when you nurse, which can make you very thirsty. Oxcytocin is the hormone responsible for the "mother-child" bond.

Mothers often worry if their baby is eating enough. With multiples it can be even more worrisome with the number of mouths that need to be fed. While your doctor is the best person to consult, a newborn often loses between five to nine percent of her birth weight but will then gain it back within the first two weeks. Newborns typically gain about an ounce a day after their fifth day in this world.

So, how often should you feed your little ones? If you are a first-time mom, you may feel it is necessary to feed your babies each time they cry. Not only is this not necessary, but with more than one mouth to feed, it may be close to impossible. A strict, fixed schedule is also not necessarily the best approach. Finding the balance between the two is essential for the well organized mom-of-multiples. While there will be some variations in time between feedings with each of your children, a general schedule will naturally evolve for each of your babies. Make note of what that schedule is, and you will be able to ascertain what your baby is asking for when she cries. Rather than being tears of hunger, she may want some cuddling or any number of other physical needs. By maintaining a flexible, but also parent-directed schedule, you and your babies can get on a schedule that brings comfort and assurance to each of your babies.

Expect each of your babies to eat every two to three hours in their first three weeks. Your babies should have about three bowel movements each day. Each of your babies will use about ten disposable diapers a day. Use the Feeding & Activity Schedule to keep track of your babies' schedule. How often they eat and release can be very indicative of health or illness.

DIAPER DUTY

While it may seem obvious, there is actually a systematic approach to changing diapers that can make the process more efficient and less traumatic for everyone involved.

Always keep each of your diaper changing stations well stocked. Before you go to bed each night, get into the habit of restocking each station. Buy your diapers (if using disposables) and baby wipes in bulk, and make sure all of the caregivers know where the bulk stash is stored.

However you choose to dispose of your diapers, diaper Genie, diaper pail, trash bin with lid, etc., keep a receptor at each of your changing stations and empty it each evening when restocking your stations.

- Breastfeeding helps bring moms and their babies closer. Even before actually breast-feeding, multiples can be fed their mother's milk by a tube. This can help mom to feel connected to her infants even before she can directly care for them herself.

Source: Breastfeeding Answer Book (La Leche International, Franklin Park, IL, 2003)

12-STEPS TO DISPOSABLE DIAPER CHANGING

1. Sanitize your hands with a wipe.

2. Make sure each of your babies are in a safe place such as their crib, playpen or on a blanket on the floor.

3. Lay your baby on your changing table or station in a safe and comfortable position. Maintain physical contact with your baby at all times. Do not ever turn away or walk away from your baby.

4. Open a clean diaper and lay it underneath the baby's soiled one.

5. Remove the straps of the diaper with baby's legs down. Take the front flap of the diaper and lay it down (unfolding it towards you). Make sure the baby's bottom is still on the back flap of the diaper.

6. Hold your baby's ankles up with one hand, so her tush is off the table but her back is still comfortably resting on the table. Remove the soiled diaper to the side.

7. Fold the dirty diaper in half with your free hand to keep the soil inside while you finish the job. Grab a baby wipe.

8. Clean your baby's penis or vagina. Be sure to wipe front to back to reduce the risk of spreading bacteria.

9. Keep baby's bottom up while you wipe the large bits of stool off. Then clean the rest of the bottom. For a really messy diaper, expect to use about four to six wipes. As you use the wipes, place the used ones on top of the soiled diaper that you just removed. You should still be holding the child's bottom up by the ankles.

10. Lower your baby gently onto the new diaper. Bring the flap forward and tape it to the back flap around the child's waist, making sure it's not too tight. Finish wrapping up the soiled diaper, placing the soiled wipes inside. Use the tabs to bundle it all tightly.

11. Dispose of the diaper in a diaper pail or tie it into a small plastic bag, and place it in an outside garbage can.

12. Wash your hands thoroughly, and wipe baby's hands with another wipe.

Good to Know

There are many great products on the market to assist moms-of-multiples with the challenges of breastfeeding multiples babies. Consult with your lactation specialist to address your specific challenges.

If you have chosen cloth diapers as your main source of diapering, the process is completely different. First, you need to know how to fold them.

FOLDING CLOTH DIAPERS

1. Prepare a clean, pre-washed diaper. Cloth diapers usually come pre-folded to 14 inches by 20 inches, but you may have to fold them more to ensure they fit you baby snugly. Most diaper services will provide pre-folded diapers, but you will need to know how to fold them as well.

2. Spread the diaper. Fold one-third of the width from the left edge toward the center.

3. Fold one-third of the width from the right edge toward the center, leaving a strip one-third the width of the original cloth. The diaper should now be three-layers thick.

4. Fold one-third up from the bottom so you have a six-ply thickness. Position this area in the front for a boy; for a girl, place it under her rear.

12 STEPS TO CLOTH DIAPER CHANGING USING A WRAP

1. Insert the clean diaper into a diaper wrap so it will be ready to go.

2. Return to the baby and unfasten the Velcro® diaper wrap tabs, but don't remove the dirty diaper yet.

3. Wipe away any stool with the diaper, taking care to cover the penis with a clean cloth or diaper if your baby is a boy.

4. Fold the dirty diaper in half under the baby, unsoiled side up.

5. Use a baby wipe or wet cloth to clean your baby's front thoroughly. For a girl, be sure to wipe from front to back—away from her vagina. This will help minimize the chance that bacteria will get into her vagina and cause an infection.

PRODUCT PICK

Check out www.DoubleB-lessings.com and www.mybrestfriend.com for a nice selection of twins nursing pillows.

6. Lift both of your baby's legs and clean her tush.

7. Switch the clean diaper for the dirty one. The clean diaper should be positioned so half of it is under your baby's bottom, and the other half between her legs.

8. When you're pulling the diaper up through her legs, pinch the fabric together so as not to be as likely to bunch, which can cause chafing and discomfort.

9. For newborns, position your child so the back of the diaper is higher than the front so the diaper will not irritate the umbilical cord (you can get special newborn diapers with notches cut out for the stump). For boys, be sure to tuck the penis down so moisture will be less likely to escape.

10. If you're using a diaper wrap, and it's not dirty, you can use it again. If it's soiled, toss it in the laundry when you are finished and grab a clean one for now.

11. If you're using a diaper wrap with Velcro® tabs, simply fasten them, making sure the diaper is snug but not so tight that it pinches your baby's skin.

12. Dispose of any stool inside the soiled diaper into the toilet. Put the used diaper in your diaper pail. If you're not using a diaper service, wash diapers in a separate load, and use soap, not detergent. Use hot water, double rinse, and avoid fabric softeners or antistatic products, as they can irritate your baby's sensitive skin.

6 STEPS TO CHANGING A CLOTH DIAPER USING PINS

1. Prepare a clean, pre-washed diaper. Before pinning, follow steps two through seven on Steps to Cloth Diaper Changing Using a Wrap.
2. Place a clean diaper under your baby. Make the flaps by flaring them out at the top of the back half of the diaper.
3. Pull the side flaps forward from back of diaper.
4. Avoid giving your baby an accidental pinprick by placing two fingers under the diaper fabric.
5. Insert the pin away from your baby's navel, and be sure

not to push it through all the layers of the inner fold of diaper.

6. Dispose of any stool in the toilet. Put the used diaper in your diaper pail. If you are not using a diaper service, wash diapers in a separate load, and use soap, not detergent. Use hot water, double rinse, and avoid fabric softeners or antistatic products, as they can irritate your baby's sensitive skin.

Source: www.babycenter.com

BE A DELEGATING DIVA

While you can't go around bossing everyone, do take full advantage when someone offers to assist you. You can't do everything and your friends and family want to help. They will appreciate the direction you provide them. This is especially true for out of town guests. They have come to be of service and not to be entertained. Allow yourself to be pampered by them.

Your parents, friends and family will need assistance in understanding exactly what you need help with. Be open and honest in explaining your needs. Do you need help personally or with the babies? Explain your parenting style so that you all feel comfortable with the support they provide. Be sure to set your expectations before the babies arrive to avoid confusion and hurt feelings in the midst of the chaos of the new babies.

While your friends and family may be a great help to you, try not to lose patience or become upset if your parenting style is challenged. Mothers, aunts, grandparents—they have all "been there before" when raising you and your siblings. If, or when, you come to a disagreement about parenting be firm about your own parenting style. Take the advice you find valuable and move forward. You may make your own mistakes, but you will also achieve your own successes.

Have the Sign Up to Assist form readily available so when someone offers to help, you will be able to assign her a task and a time right there on the spot. The following is a list of tasks that are easily delegated:

- Wash and sterilize bottles
- Feed babies (especially late night and early morning feedings)
- Bathe babies
- Play with and care for older children
- Take older children to school and assist with homework and extra-curricular events
- Care for pets
- Do grocery shopping
- Processing mail
- Prepare meals
- Wash dishes and clean the house
- Run errands
- Wash and fold laundry
- Care for babies while mommy rests
- Assist with doctor visits
- Care for at-home baby if you still have babies in the NICU

CONNECT TO YOUR CALM PLACE

Parenting singletons is not for the faint of heart. However, parenting multiples is much like being a superhero. Have you noticed all superheroes have special accoutrements that give them power; they have an outside source that works through them. You can be a superhero too when you connect to your calm place.

Empower yourself through daily meditation, prayer, affirmations and/or visualizations. Make it a daily ritual to connect with your faith, which is where you will miraculously find the energy, strength, patience and fortitude to embrace and excel as a parent. You will be amazed at what you can accomplish.

Start each morning and end each day with a prayer or meditation. In his book, The Seven Spiritual Laws of Success, Deepak Chopra advises a thirty-minute meditation each morning and each evening. Your meditation can be a faith-based connection to your higher power, or a meditation of self-reflection and encouragement. Wherever you find your strength, connect with that source ritually.

If you did not exercise before your pregnancy, you will find great strength and rejuvenation in an exercise program. Yoga and Pilates are both disciplines that will strengthen your mind, body and spirit. You can join a gym and take a group class, have private instruction in your own home or purchase a DVD exercise series. There are even Yoga programs for infants, toddlers and children so you can introduce these disciplines to your children in infancy, which can grow into a healthful opportunity for quality family togetherness.

Walking each day is another easy and meditative exercise you can enjoy with your children. Family walks through the neighborhood, as well as local nature trails are great ways to connect with your spouse while connecting to your calm place.

Music provides another avenue of connecting with your spirit. Mozart is especially beneficial. Choose music that enriches your spirit and is uplifting to your mood. Music is a very powerful influence over our minds and moods. Choose calming music that is restful and assists in connecting to your spirit.

Good to Know

Keep an ongoing list of people who you need to thank. Whether it is for their time or a gift. Try to write and send five cards a day.

FORMS
• Sign Up To Assist

ADDITIONAL RESOURCES
• www.babycenter.com
• www.kangaroomothercare.com
• www.SendOutCards.com/27556
• www.winsorpilates.com
• www.gaiam.com
• www.anonymousone.com

SIGN UP TO ASSIST

Use the Sign Up To Assist form to ensure you have ample help on hand when your babies arrive.

DAILY HOUSEHOLD CLEANUP

Time	Monday	Tuesday	Wednesday	Thursday	Friday	Saturday	Sunday
7:00 am							
7:30 am							
8:00 am							
8:30 am							
9:00 am	Jan		Jan		Jan		
9:30 am							
10:00 am							
10:30 am							
11:00 am	Teri	Teri	Teri	Teri	Teri		
11:30 am	Teri	Teri	Teri	Teri	Teri		
12:00 pm							
12:30 pm							
1:00 pm							
1:30 pm							
2:00 pm	Heather	Heather	Heather	Heather	Heather	Heather	Heather
2:30 pm							
3:00 pm							
3:30 pm							
4:00 pm							
4:30 pm							
5:00 pm	Teri	Teri	Teri	Teri	Teri	Teri	Teri
5:30 pm							
6:00 pm	Grandma		Julie	Julie		Grandma	Grandma
6:30 pm	Grandma		Julie	Julie		Grandma	Grandma
7:00 pm							

Chapter 8
Routine, Routine, Routine

Confidence for mom and for babies comes when everyone knows what to expect. By developing and committing to a schedule for feedings, napping and play activities your babies will begin to naturally adopt the routine. Developing a routine also assists in the development of emotional security. Babies find great comfort in knowing "what's next" versus living a life full of daily surprises. At first, you may struggle with the routine, which may feel monotonous and rigid, but stay with it! Once you commit to your schedule, you will find it is complete chaos if you get outside of it—even for one day.

A lack of routine and predictability will be chaotic—for you and your babies. You will be stressed, tired, frustrated and far from operating at your best. From the earliest age, even in utero, your babies will sense your mood and your attitude. If you are exhausted and frustrated, your children will respond in a similar way, making your job as the parent twice (or three or four times) as hard.

As a parent, when you set an example of modeling a routine, you are providing daily lessons of discipline. As infants, your babies will find comfort and confidence in a routine. As they grow older, the practice of a routine will benefit them tremendously with regard to academics, sports and moral development. Routine teaches children to "stay with it." Children who are raised around a consistent routine are more likely to understand the importance and pay-off of following through with commitments, whether it is a commitment to a sports team or commitment to learn a new instrument. In areas where practice is essential to a successful accomplishment, a child raised in a routine will have a far greater chance of developing persistence and tenacity.

FEEDING

Parents of multiples must take control of the feeding schedule for their babies. This is the most important routine to establish, as it will impact all other routines in your household. I highly recommend the "parent-directed feeding" approach presented by Gary and Annie Marie Ezzo in their Preparation for Parenting: Along the Infant Way. Ezzo and Ezzo define parent-directed feeding as, "… a twenty-four hour infant management strategy designed to help moms connect with their babies and their babies to them." This proactive approach to infant care meets not only the babies' needs, but also the needs of the entire family.

Parent-directed feeding is guided by both hunger cues, as well as a timed schedule. Simply put, a developmentally appropriate feeding schedule is implemented, but the parent assesses the true need for a feeding when the baby elicits a hunger cue outside of that schedule. This is a child-oriented approach rather than a child-focused or mother-focused approach. By utilizing this approach both mom and babies learn to cooperate with one another. The babies' needs are met without developing an on-demand approach to mom fulfilling babies' needs.

Utilize the Feeding Schedule form that accompanies this chapter. A sample schedule is provided, as well as a blank form for your own use.

SLEEPING

The parent-directed feeding strategy is closely tied to the babies' sleeping schedules. Parent-directed feeding is designed to meet your babies' needs for environmental structure, as well as her need for emotional security. This approach allows for routine and predictability around feeding and sleeping. When your babies' nutritional needs are met consistently and routinely, their sleeping patterns will naturally and rhythmically evolve around a content tummy. By using the feeding schedule, you are able to mold the sleeping patterns of your babies to meet your lifestyle needs. You will also be able to obtain consistent, uninterrupted sleep, which in turn makes you a more patient and confident mom who is parenting well-adjusted, confident babies.

ACTIVITIES

Keeping your babies activities consistent and on a routine is also essential. Once your babies get beyond the newborn phase of perpetual sleeping, you will quickly learn they can only hold their attention on one activity for about ten to fifteen minutes. By developing a routine of activities, they will naturally adopt the routine and will actually become fussy if their routine is interrupted, versus the opposite, which is continuous fussiness due to a lack of routine.

Because babies have a short attention span, their activities should be limited to fifteen-minute increments or units. Fortunately, this means it is not necessary to have two (or three, or four) of everything. While one baby is swinging, another baby can be in "tummy-time" while the third baby is having playpen-time. Use the sample Activity Schedule form and blank Activity Schedule form provided to create a customized daily activities schedule for your babies and your family.

SIGN UP FOR SIGNING

Developing early communication skills with your babies will greatly reduce the number of unnecessary tantrums associated with the frustration infants feel due to their inability to effectively communicate. Learning early communication skills will also eliminate the perpetual guessing game that exists between your babies and their caregivers. Children can actually learn to communicate through American Sign Language (ASL).

Babies who learn ASL have a tendency to speak sooner and with larger vocabularies. As compared to their non-signing counterparts, they tend to have an increased intelligence quotient while also engaging in more sophisticated play. And, multiples who sign are also able to communicate more effectively with one another, which can result in fewer sibling spats. ASL also allows your older singleton children to communicate with their baby brothers and or sisters, which enhances their own bond with their siblings. As babies grow into toddlers, their sophisticated communication capabilities greatly reduce the tantrums associated with the terrible twos.

Good to Know

If your babies do not immediately grasp the concept of signing (which they probably won't), don't give up. Some babies do not fully grasp the concept until 12 months of age. We consistently practiced signing from seven months on, and finally around 10–11 months both our girls "got" what we were trying to teach them! I thought, "Gosh, they aren't understanding what I am trying to accomplish." But, they were processing everything. Just keep at it … you will thank yourselves later.

Signing With Baby Resources

Baby Signing Time: Available at signingtime.com

Baby Einstein: My First Signs: Available at Amazon.com

Wee Hands. Visit www.weehands.com to sign-up for a class near you.

Just as all babies learn to speak at different ages, babies will also begin to sign at varying ages. As soon as possible, begin learning the signs and use them with your babies at all times. As you speak to them, also sign to them. Most babies do not yet have the motor skills necessary to begin signing themselves until nine to ten months. However, they will show interest and will begin learning the meanings of the signs much earlier; so don't wait until they are nine months old to introduce the concept to them.

Classes, DVDs and books are available to teach the basics. Also, look on the Internet for Web sites that provide additional information. Mybabycantalk.com is a great site to get you started.

FORMS

- Feeding Schedule form
- Activity Schedule form

ADDITIONAL RESOURCES

- Let The Children Come Along The Way (series) by Gary Ezzo & Anne Marie Ezzo
- One Becoming Baby Wise by Gary Ezzo and Robert Bucknam
- www.signingbaby.com

FEEDING SCHEDULE

CHAOS 2 CALM

	Feedings/Diapers									
	1	2	3	4	5	6	7	8	9	
Targeted Time	7:00 am	10:00 am	1:00 pm	4:00 pm	7:00 pm					TOTALS
Actual Time										
Monday	R=	R=	R=	R=	R=					
Date: ___/___/___	L=	L=	L=	L=	L=					
R= Right Breast L= Left Breast	#Wet	#Wet	#Wet	#Wet	#Wet	#Wet	#Wet	#Wet		
	#Poop	#Poop	#Poop	#Poop	#Poop	#Poop	#Poop	#Poop		
Targeted Time	7:00 am	10:00 am	1:00 pm	4:00 pm	7:00 pm					TOTALS
Actual Time										
Tuesday	R=	R=	R=	R=	R=					
Date: ___/___/___	L=	L=	L=	L=	L=					
R= Right Breast L= Left Breast	#Wet	#Wet	#Wet	#Wet	#Wet	#Wet	#Wet	#Wet		
	#Poop	#Poop	#Poop	#Poop	#Poop	#Poop	#Poop	#Poop		
Targeted Time	7:00 am	10:00 am	1:00 pm	4:00 pm	7:00 pm					TOTALS
Actual Time										
Wednesday	R=	R=	R=	R=	R=					
Date: ___/___/___	L=	L=	L=	L=	L=					
R= Right Breast L= Left Breast	#Wet	#Wet	#Wet	#Wet	#Wet	#Wet	#Wet	#Wet		
	#Poop	#Poop	#Poop	#Poop	#Poop	#Poop	#Poop	#Poop		
Targeted Time	7:00 am	10:00 am	1:00 pm	4:00 pm	7:00 pm					TOTALS
Actual Time										
Thursday	R=	R=	R=	R=	R=					
Date: ___/___/___	L=	L=	L=	L=	L=					
R= Right Breast L= Left Breast	#Wet	#Wet	#Wet	#Wet	#Wet	#Wet	#Wet	#Wet		
	#Poop	#Poop	#Poop	#Poop	#Poop	#Poop	#Poop	#Poop		
Targeted Time	7:00 am	10:00 am	1:00 pm	4:00 pm	7:00 pm					TOTALS
Actual Time										
Friday	R=	R=	R=	R=	R=					
Date: ___/___/___	L=	L=	L=	L=	L=					
R= Right Breast L= Left Breast	#Wet	#Wet	#Wet	#Wet	#Wet	#Wet	#Wet	#Wet		
	#Poop	#Poop	#Poop	#Poop	#Poop	#Poop	#Poop	#Poop		
Targeted Time	7:00 am	10:00 am	1:00 pm	4:00 pm	7:00 pm					TOTALS
Actual Time										
Saturday	R=	R=	R=	R=	R=					
Date: ___/___/___	L=	L=	L=	L=	L=					
R= Right Breast L= Left Breast	#Wet	#Wet	#Wet	#Wet	#Wet	#Wet	#Wet	#Wet		
	#Poop	#Poop	#Poop	#Poop	#Poop	#Poop	#Poop	#Poop		
Targeted Time	7:00 am	10:00 am	1:00 pm	4:00 pm	7:00 pm					TOTALS
Actual Time										
Sunday	R=	R=	R=	R=	R=					
Date: ___/___/___	L=	L=	L=	L=	L=					
R= Right Breast L= Left Breast	#Wet	#Wet	#Wet	#Wet	#Wet	#Wet	#Wet	#Wet		
	#Poop	#Poop	#Poop	#Poop	#Poop	#Poop	#Poop	#Poop		

ACTIVITY SCHEDULE

7:00 am

7:30 am

8:00 am

8:30 am

9:00 am

9:30 am

10:00 am

10:30 am

11:00 am

11:30 am

12:00 pm

12:30 pm

1:00 pm

1:30 pm

2:00 pm

2:30 pm

3:00 pm

3:30 pm

4:00 pm

4:30 pm

5:00 pm

5:30 pm

6:00 pm

6:30 pm

7:00 pm

Chapter 9

The Terrific Twos Times Two

Organization plays a much deeper role in family life than what one may initially think. A well organized home, family and life is much more than maintaining orderly cabinets and closets. Organization speaks to the very core of your family values.

How can you teach a child to care for her toys and books, when the kitchen is a mess? How can you teach a child manners, when your schedule is so disorganized family dinners happen only at Easter, Christmas and Thanksgiving, and usually at someone else's house? How can you teach a child practical life skills, when the only organization that occurs in the house is done by the housekeeper? How can you teach a child personal safety, when you are tripping over your own piles of laundry, shoes and briefcases?

We all want to raise children who grow into well-mannered, self-composed adults who are able to be a contribution to society. Believe it or not, the foundation for this is found in consistent and persistent organization. If you are not currently living a life of order and organization, start now! You may even want to employ an expert to help you. Professional Organizers and Life Coaches are experts in bringing order and direction to the lives of individuals and their families. So, let's take a look at how this will impact your multiple toddlers.

TURN THE TERRIBLE TWOS INTO TERRIFIC TWOS!

Routine serves as rules in infancy. The world of exploration for an infant lies within the boundaries of her own little arm. If she can reach it, she can explore it. Her routine is what will be the greatest influence on her behavior. As a matter of fact, barring illness or discomfort, your babies' behavior is a direct reflection of the routine, or lack there of, that you have implemented. Toddlers, on the other hand, require steadfast rules in order to keep them safe and developing emotionally and behaviorally in a manner that is consistent with your family values.

By completing the Family Core Values form found in chapter one, you and your spouse will have clearly communicated, and hopefully agreed upon, what your family's values are and how they should be demonstrated within your family and society. So, with that in mind, remember that your actions will always speak louder than your words ever can. If you want your children to show respect to animals, you must show respect to animals—always. If you want your child to eat her vegetables, you better eat your vegetables. If you want your child to speak kindly and respectfully to you, you must speak kindly and respectfully to her—always. The key to instilling your family's values within the character of your children is modeling that behavior with as few exceptions as possible.

Commit to a monthly meeting with your spouse to revisit your Family Core Values. This will help you to agree upon changes in circumstances or viewpoints as they are presented in your family. Just like most aspects of parenting, this will remain a work in progress. My husband and I have done this since the twins were born and it has been a great help in our accountability with one another as our twins grow and we as parents are faced with new challenges.

Just like walking, learning sign language, and speaking, learning "the rules" is a process. When your toddlers err in behavior, gently but firmly, and always consistently, remind them of the proper behavior and move on. Always phrase your correction in the positive. So rather than say, "Emma, do not hit your brother;" say, "Emma, please be kind and gentle with your brother." In this way, your focus is on the positive behavior you would like to see her demonstrate versus the negative behavior you want her to eliminate.

HELP YOUR TODDLERS HELP THEMSELVES

Toddlers crave independence. Their brains are rapidly developing, as are their motor skills. All too often, parents discourage independence either from a belief that their toddlers are incapable of completing the task at hand or from a lack of patience. Yes, it will take your toddler more time to take his pajamas off and put them away in a drawer, but he can do it. And, he wants to do it.

Another prohibitive factor in allowing toddlers to be independent is that they will create a bigger mess in the process. For instance, your toddler can place the toothpaste on his own toothbrush, but he will probably get it on himself, his pajamas, the counter and his toothbrush. While it can certainly be annoying and time-consuming, be careful to not deny your toddler every opportunity for developing practical life skills. Practice does make perfect, and when he is three, four, five ... and eighteen, you will thank yourself for instilling the independence and self-esteem to go on and accomplish great things. Becoming adept at simple practical life skills is a process, but it is an essential process, especially when caring for multiples.

ADDITIONAL RESOURCE

- www.michaelolaf.com provides a wealth of information and practical life materials for parents and teachers to help their toddler learn independence and self-care.

Chapter 10

Mother Nature's Baby
By Christy Ilfrey, Co-owner
of NativeDave.com

When my husband and I learned we were expecting our first child, we knew we would pass along our planet-focused values. Long before our little NativeBabe, we were working and living by the five Rs: reduce, reuse, recycle, re-buy and replace. We co-own a small business founded on principles of sustainability; our business is an extension of our personalities and souls. The green principles that guide us, we discovered, certainly had prepared us for raising a green baby.

Overall, we both have healthy eating habits. A few weeks before The Big News arrived I had begun transitioning toward a mostly raw food diet. I met an enthusiastic "raw foodie" at a local Earth Day event who raved about the benefits of her lifestyle. I had to admit, her complexion was clear and smooth, and her eyes were bright with vitality. She recommended I read Victoria Boutenko's Green for Life. I did, and was instantly inspired to drink at least one "green smoothie" per day. Leafy green vegetables such as spinach, kale and celery all contain an abundance of vitamins and minerals. In her book, Boutenko explains that our jaws have weakened over generations and cannot adequately masticate greens. Therefore, to be able to release the nutrients bound in plant cellulose—and render them a palatable, consumable form—she recommends processing greens in a high-speed blender. Uncertain about taste and consistency, I was apprehensive about sampling one of Boutenko's many recipes. Amazingly, it didn't taste "earthy" or raw. Combined properly, raw ingredients provide a surprisingly rich and complex palette of flavors and textures.

Next, I moved on to Natalia Rose's, The Raw Food Detox Diet. What I like about her advice is that it is relevant to "Level One" raw foodies as well as Level Five meat-and-potato eaters. The more raw food meals one integrates into her existing diet, I came to understand, the more she will trade the burgers and fries for natural foods. Foods like Sweet Potato-Carrot Bisque served with sprouted grain bread dispel the myth that raw food equals flavorless cuisine. The notion that I could heal myself from the inside with flavorful, nutrient-dense foods intrigued me.

Over those few weeks I developed an almost spiritual connection to salads without dressing, raw juices and the miracles I could perform with my Blendtec Ultimate Blender (Available at www.totalblender.com). My taste buds leaped excitedly in celebration of Green Lemonade and all the raw fruit I could fuse. Everything I consumed made my brain buzz, alive with energy released from these magical concoctions.

And then we received the news: baby will make three.

Typically I prefer to eat a plant-based diet supplemented occasionally with fish. I am an advocate for animal rights. I agree with studies that conclude that animal-based diets lack proper nutrition, cause health problems long-term and impose on the planet's natural resources. Although I consider myself a politically astute person, my preference for fruits, vegetables, nuts and seeds, and grains is no political statement. It is simply what I like. During my pregnancy my body has had difficulty absorbing non-heme (plant-based) iron; I'm flirting with anemia. Therefore, for the baby's safety and mine, I have had to incorporate heme (meat-based) iron. Red meat and other meats cooked in cast iron cookware have supplemented my mostly-plant regimen. When baby arrives, I plan to phase out the animal foodstuffs.

I plan to serve our little NativeBabe homemade baby food made with organic fruits and vegetables. I have already been preparing Baby by drinking daily fruit smoothies and occasional green smoothies. The process is quite easy and economical.

ECO-FRIENDLY BABY FOOD

If you do not already have one, you will need to purchase a high-speed blender, as well as some ice trays. Pour the blended ingredients into ice trays and freeze them. Defrost the "cubes" in the refrigerator, and then serve to baby.

The Environmental Working Group (EWG) recently found that not all conventional foods endanger our well being. While some expose us to dangerous levels of carcinogens, others present only limited risks. On the Gaiam Community Web site are two lists: one that ranks the twelve foods with highest chemical residue, and the other ranks the twelve with the lowest residue. Those on the "highest residue" should always be purchased in organic form. The "lowest residue" items can safely be consumed in conventional form. If you're like me and must prioritize your organic purchases, these lists are priceless.

We could purchase fresh, raw (preferably organic) produce from our local grocer. But why not grow our own? Regardless of the size of our property, it is possible to grow plentiful edible plants. Containers—pottery, window boxes, etc.—make excellent "trial gardens." This year I grew basil, rosemary, mint and cherry tomatoes—all are grown in clay pots without chemicals and with minimal watering. As a matter of fact, my plants have been "trained" to be almost self-sufficient. Next year, I hope to have a larger space to raise more varieties of vegetables and fruits.

Easy and more economical than store brands, homemade baby food can be the pinnacle of nutrition nirvana for baby. Both Vegetarian Baby and Child Online Magazine offer plenty of recipes for baby food. "Wholesome Baby Foods from Scratch," found in the recipes section of The Vegetarian Resource Group's Web site describes necessary equipment and methods for making clean, healthy and delicious food for baby. Several Web sites tout the So Easy Baby Food Kit

PRODUCT PICK

The Organic Baby & Toddler Cookbook (Organic) by Lizzie Vann and Daphne Razazan is a wonderful guide for cooking green for your babies. Available at www.Amazon.com.

PRODUCT PICK

The Deceptively Delicious by Jessica Seinfeld provides great recipes for sneaking greens in your children's diet. Available at www.Amazon.com.

PRODUCT PICK

Earth's Best baby foods are organically grown in soil that is not contaminated with harmful pesticides. They use only whole grains, fruits and vegetables that are nutrient-rich and full of flavor. Earth's Best never adds sugar, salt, starches, fillers or preservatives.

as "a complete solution for making healthy, all-natural baby food at home in less than 30 minutes per week.

ECO-FASHION FOR MOMMY & BABY

To minimize external, or dermal, contact with synthetic chemicals, I have gradually replaced clothing made from conventionally grown cotton and synthetics with those constructed with sustainable fibers. Conventional cotton accounts for one-quarter of all the agricultural insecticides applied globally each year; it is the most pesticide-intensive crop grown on the planet. Many of these chemicals are known carcinogens. Workers in cotton fields around the world have reported neurological and vision disorders, chromosomal aberrations and many other physical and cellular augmentations. Juvenile and pet cancers are on the rise where parents consistently use synthetic pesticides in their homes and/or gardens. Thousands of people die each year from pesticide poisoning. If we purchase and wear cotton clothing, we are draping pesticide-laden fabrics over our bodies.

I do not recommend tossing out everything to make way for organic garb. But as pieces become worn, I replace them with items constructed with organic cotton, hemp, bamboo or soy. Worn clothing is "free-cycled" (www.freecycle.org) or donated to charitable organizations. Damaged clothing may go to seamstresses creating reconstructed fashions.

Recently, more organic and sustainable clothing products have entered the online shopping scene. Styles now range from traditional neo-hippie to corporate executive, and everything in between. Trendy as well as timeless pieces are readily available. No longer are we limited to organic garments in white or natural. Thanks to plant-based dyes, socially conscious clothing comes in a variety of vibrant colors. Increased competition in the marketplace has also brought prices down so that average-income families may afford these items. Wal-Mart has become the world's number one purchaser of organic cotton, and Target has a fabulous organic clothing line specifically for infants.

Surprisingly, one of the best resources for organic clothing at reasonable prices is eBay. Stores like Natural

Living and Rage Baby Clothing offer high-quality clothing for the entire family. For maternity wear, I have been eyeing Kid Bean's Organic Cotton Plus Cup Nursing Bras in snazzy colors, like blueberry, blackberry and chocolate. According to my thrifty pregnant friends, a nursing bra may double as a maternity bra. Round Belly's organic floral blouse in sunflower yellow-and-white would make any woman happy to be pregnant in summer. Perhaps my favorite find is MollyAna Maternity's organic maternity tees. Other must-check-out lines are Blue Canoe and Under the Nile; more options are becoming available every day.

Online retailers, like Kate Quinn Organics and Sckoon, offer Asian-infused, gender-neutral options for baby. Kid Bean, Progressive Kid and Round Belly carry plenty of receiving blankets, burp blankets, and baby clothes sewn with organic cotton. Eco Baby Organics puts it all together: clothing, bedding, toys, and even organic cotton diapers. For hemp diapers, try Tiny Tush Natural Baby Boutique, Crickett's Diapers or Rawganique. Rawganique's inventory of organic clothing for mommy and daddy is quite extensive as well.

ECO-PLAY

Perhaps the most accessible organic baby items are toys. I bought organic cotton veggies by Under the Nile for a friend's son on his first birthday. According to my friend, her son cannot keep them out of his mouth—that's a great review from a baby! I liked them so much I added them to my baby's registry. Other online vendors I found are Sum-Bo-Shine, Alternative Baby, Nature's Crib and The Playstore.

KEEPING IT ALL ECO-CLEAN

My husband and I agreed we would use cloth diapers instead of disposables. Many times we have observed first-hand the horror that is our local landfill, and we refuse to contribute to the problem. We selected organic cotton diapers with snap-closure diaper covers by Bummis. Biodegradable, flushable diaper liners make clean up easier. A small hand-held nozzle attached to your bathroom sink cleans up baby and diaper in seconds.

All new garments, diapers and toys are washed with non-toxic detergents before we wear them or put them away for baby. Biokleen and Mrs. Meyers are two of my favorite brands. There are, however, more people- and planet-friendly laundry products than ever before. Many brands also manufacture dish washing liquid and detergents; some even formulate cleaning products. I have had great results with most of them, but for most housekeeping tasks—unclogging drains; removing soap scum; and scrubbing toilets, bathtubs, and sinks, for example—baking soda and white vinegar work just fine. Vinegar cleans mirrors and glass surfaces without smearing, and it is also a powerful disinfectant.

Together, baking soda and vinegar trigger a reaction just volatile enough to unclog drains. Once-per-month I put approximately half a cup to one cup of baking soda into every drain in my house, followed by two to three cups of white distilled vinegar. As the foam recedes down the drain—carrying hair and other sink sludge with it—I chase it with a quart or so of boiling water. This drain cleaning method is much safer for humans and pets than synthetic store-bought products, and it does not contaminate local water resources.

Counter tops and appliances may be wiped down with vinegar. My favorite all-purpose cleaner, however, is Orange TKO. It is organic, has a citrus fragrance and, because it is concentrated, will last a long time. In addition to cleaning counter tops and appliances, I use it to dust wood furniture, to remove scuff marks on baseboards, and to mop tile and linoleum floors.

ECO-PLAYGROUND

Managing our outdoor environment organically—for us and for baby—is equally important. Most homeowners maintain a lawn, vast expanses of turf grass that are watered, fertilized, sprayed with chemicals and mown. The lawn is the most wasteful element in the landscape, and the most toxic to humans and pets. Exposure to synthetic chemicals may cause illness or even death. Homeowners tend not to follow directions, thereby increasing susceptibility to medical issues. Numerous studies have established a direct link between consistent exposure to synthetic lawn and household chemicals and various medical issues, such as childhood cancers, pet bladder cancer, breast cancer, and infertility. Citations are listed at www.chem-tox.com/pesticides.

For our family, the solution is simple: eradicate the lawn by increasing planting beds and selecting local native plants. Properly choreographed native planting beds survive on ambient rainfall and without synthetic chemicals. Allow plants to grow into their natural form, which reduces maintenance requirements and attracts wildlife. Fertilize with compost and local native mulch.

Our NativeBabe will bring many changes to our life soon. Fortunately, we will not need to adopt "healthier" practices; our inherent green values will provide a clean, healthy environment fit for us as well as our newborn.

ADDITIONAL RESOURCES

- Shaklee makes wonderful non-toxic, eco-friendly household, laundry and kitchen cleaners that are biodegradable and safe for the earth, your babies and your entire family. Available at www.shaklee.net/sortedout.

- California Baby offers an extensive line of all natural products for the natural baby. From full body care to essential oils, totes and accessories, this online boutique has it all! www.californiababy.com.

- Visit http://community.gaiam.com/ for more information about eco-living.

- Freecycle.org is a fantastic Web site to dispose of items you no longer need, as well as to obtain items (for free) that you may need.

Chapter 11

Babies On The Go

The key to successful outings with your babies is preparation, organization and prevention. Make it a ritual to always bring the diaper bag in from the car each time you come and go. Empty any garbage or dirty diapers that may have accumulated after each outing. At the end of the day, restock your diaper bag with all of your traveling essentials. Keep your bag well organized so that you always know what you have with you and what you need to restock. Keep your wipes, diapers, cell phone, pacifiers, etc. in the same pocket or compartment each time you use them so you are not always digging around in your bag. You will want to be able to quickly reach in your bag and know exactly where the pacifier is when your babies start to fret. By always being prepared and organized, you will be able to prevent disasters such as overloaded diapers, soiled clothing, hungry babies and any other number of things that can wreak havoc on your outing.

BABIES' FIRST WHEELS

Unfortunately, there is no perfect stroller for all multiples. Fortunately, there is a plethora of options! First decide what features are most important for your use. Consider the following when shopping for your stroller system:

- Look for strength. Strollers for multiples will obviously require more weight tolerance than strollers for singletons.

- Look for larger wheels for a more comfortable ride and ease in pushing.

- Sacrifice economy. The stroller is not the item that should be chosen based on cost. This is not only an essential item, but also one where safety should be the number one purchasing priority.

- Consider the weight of the stroller and the ease of loading into a van or a car trunk.

There are several types of strollers:

- Convertible carriage/strollers are convenient for small babies, not as convenient for toddlers.

- Side-by-Side strollers provide a separate area for each baby. Side-by-sides are twice as wide as a single stroller, and may not fit through single doors or aisles, but these are nice as the children can see and interact with one another.

- Tandem strollers allow for face-to-face seating, sharing legroom or one in front of the other. One design has the back seat slightly higher than the front so that both children have clear views. These strollers are narrow enough to easily navigate through doorways.

- There are many safe and sturdy triplet models available. Check out www.tripletconnection.org to receive information about purchasing a used stroller.

DIAPER BAG CHECKLIST
BIRTH–6 MONTHS

- 4 diapers per child
- 20 wipes per child
- 1 tube of rash ointment
- 1 changing pad
- 1 change of clothing per child
- 1 washcloth per child in a zip lock baggie
- Antiseptic wipes or gel
- 1 burp cloth per child

- 1 receiving blanket per child
- 1 bottle of formula per child
- 2 bibs per child
- 1 hat per child
- 1 waterproof disposable camera
- 1 toy or book per child
- Baby pain medicine such as Tylenol
- Mylicon
- Teething toys (1 per child)
- Teething gel

6 MONTHS–24 MONTHS

- 4 diapers per child
- 20 wipes per child
- 1 tube of rash ointment
- 1 changing pad
- 1 change of clothing per child
- 1 pair of socks per child
- 1 wash cloth per child in a zip lock baggie
- Anti-septic wipes or gel
- 1 burp cloth per child
- 1 receiving blanket per child
- 1 bottle of formula per child
- 1 sippy cup, spoon and bowl per child
- Snacks
- 2 bibs per child
- 1 hat per child
- 1 waterproof disposable camera
- 1 toy or book per child
- Small first aid kit
- Teething gel

PARENTS' GUIDE
TO TRAVELING WITH MULTIPLES

Traveling with multiples is often a combination of chaos and comedy. You will certainly want to be well prepared for the task. I highly recommend not attempting to travel solo. Always bring your spouse, grandparent, friend or even nanny along for the travel portion of the trip, if not the entire journey.

The day before you are scheduled to leave for your trip, go to www.faa.com to check carry on guidelines. Also visit your airline carrier's site to review their guidelines and recommendations for air travel with children.

If possible, schedule your flight during the time your babies usually nap. By keeping them on their regular napping schedule they will be more likely to sleep at least a portion of the trip. Keep their schedule the same as always. Trying to sleep deprive your children in hopes of catching long naps on the plane backfires more often than not.

Call ahead of time to ensure your departure time has not been delayed. You will certainly want to minimize as much waiting around time as possible. Try to schedule seating in the bulkhead where your family will have more space. If the bulkhead is not available, request a place directly over the engines. The sound of the engines serves a double purpose of lulling your children to sleep, as well as providing a sound barrier between you and your fellow travelers.

Transport your babies through the airport in their stroller and check the stroller at the gate. Be sure to arrive early enough to ensure this possibility. Prior to boarding give each of your babies one last diaper change so that they get on board fresh and clean. Your fellow travelers will also appreciate this gesture. If you babies have special blankets or other comfort items, bring these along as well. Changes in their environment are very stimulating, and they will seek comfort in these items. Once you are seated, get neighborly with your fellow passengers. They will be less likely to become disgruntled if you have befriended them.

Good to Know

Once your children are old enough to reach for things, keep a bin of soft toys and soft books in a small bin between the car seats. This bin can easily be moved to the trunk in the event you need the passenger space.

CARRY-ON DIAPER BAG

Packing a diaper bag for air travel requires some additions to your standard diaper bag must-haves. Don't store your diaper bag in the overhead compartment. You will need quick and easy access to the following items:

- Keep at least 4 diapers per child on hand in the diaper bag along with wipes and rash cream.
- Pack several freezer-size zip lock baggies for soiled diapers.
- Antibacterial wipes or gel.
- Enough powder formula to make two bottles per child.
- Two changes of clothes for each child.
- An extra top for you in case of spit-up.
- Diaper changing pad.
- Snacks
- Several burp cloths
- Toys and books

ELIMINATING EAR PAIN

The shifts in altitude, especially on take-off and landing, can cause ear pain in both adults and infants. Since your babies cannot yet chew gum, offer them a pacifier, as the sucking will help to alleviate some of the pain. Have a bottle or sippy cup on hand in case your baby will not take the pacifier. Several days prior to traveling, be extra careful to make sure your babies are well hydrated, and never travel if your children have ear infections. The shift in altitude can cause severe damage to their inner ears and may even cause their eardrums to rupture.

The safest method of flying for babies is in a FAA-approved car seat. Check with your airline in advance to confirm that your brand of car seat is compatible with their seats.

PRODUCT PICK

These back seat car organizers are perfect for keeping all of your essentials organized while you are on the go. www.stacksandstacks.com

WHAT TO PACK
& WHAT TO PURCHASE

There are certain items you will need to pack, but you can save space by purchasing consumable goods once you arrive your destination.

PACK
- Car seat for each child (preferably one with rollers)
- Sippy Cups
- Bibs: 2 bids per child, per day
- Pack-N-Play: 1 per child

PURCHASE
- Food
- Formula
- Diapers
- Wipes

Traveling with multiples is not necessarily easy, but can be lots of fun. Just remember to take all the little "hick-ups" in stride and remember even the big snafus will make for a funny story someday!

Epilogue

Our twins are now 21 months old, and organization has become a way of life for these two little ones already. I marvel at their dependence on organization, structure and routine. You always hear about the importance of appreciating every moment. All of my friends, family and fellow mothers-of-multiples always told me to enjoy every second because they grow up fast. Don't ever wish they are older or bigger, you can't ever get that back! Now I am sitting her writing this, and they are almost two. It's truly amazing how fast time has gone. Before you know it, your babies will be as mobile as mine. You will thank yourself later for being organized, because they get into everything and keep you running. Whether you are a stay-at-home mom, stay-at-home dad, working mother or single mother, I assure you, being consistent and being organized will help you save time, which in turn gives you more time to enjoy your babies.

Enjoy your new blessed journey with your new miracles!

Additional Resources

CHAPTER 1

1. Baby to Bee is a Web site every expecting parent should utilize. Download coupons, get freebies, get advice on current products and receive helpful tips. www.babytobee.com

2. Planning Family offers free samples, product offers, coupons, and sweepstakes from well known brands. www.planningfamily.com

3. Order discounted diapers (and much more) and receive free shipping from www.diapers.com.

4. Mr. Rebates (www.mrrebates.com) offers a vast variety of home and baby products. Every purchase earns you cash back.

5. From birth announcements to strollers, Just Multiples offers a wide variety of products specifically for parents of multiples. www.justmultiples.com

6. BabyCenter.com provides helpful tips and general month-by-month expectations for pregnancy.

7. The National Organization of Mother of Twins Club, Inc. www.nomotc.org

8. MOST (Mothers of Supertwins) is a wonderful organization that provides support to "Multiple Birth Families ... Every Step of the Way." www.mostonline.org

SUGGESTED READING

1. Twice Upon A Time: Twin baby memories by Lynn Lorenz

2. Expecting Multiples DVD Course: DVD 1 - Preparing for Multiples with Nutrition & Preventative Care; DVD 2 - The Birth Experience & Life with Multiples

3. Sweet Jasmine, Nice Jackson ~ What It's Like To Be 2-And To Be Twins! by Robie H. Harris and Michael Emberley

4. Subscribe to Twins Magazine as soon as you learn you are pregnant with multiples. www.twinsmagazine.com

5. Twin to Twin by Margaret O'Hair and Thierry Courtin

6. TwinsTalk.com is a great resource for parent-to-parent advice.

CHAPTER 2

1. International Association For Child Safety- www.iafcs.com

2. Safe Kids Worldwide- www.safekids.org

3. American Academy of Pediatrics- www.aap.org

4. International Association For Child Safety- http://69.13.128.173/findachildproofer.asp

CHAPTER 3

1. Twinzgear.com offers unique and hard to find twins items for every member of the family. From shower gifts, nursing pillows, clothing, gifts for the family of twins, and even "Twingles" items for mothers of twins and a singleton, this store provides many of the must-have items. And, it is owned and operated by a family with twins, so they know what parents of multiples really need.

2. Just4Twins.com is a great Web site for all things twins: cute t-shirts, onesies, ball caps, etc.

3. Chat online with other moms-of-multiples at twinstuff.com.

4. Tinyprints.com is a fantastic online store for custom invitation.

CHAPTER 4

1. Care.com is a great Web site for parents seeking in-home nanny care. Just type in your zip code and start searching for caregivers in your area. www.care.com

CHAPTER 6

1. KnockKnock.biz sells fun and creative Thank You cards.

2. GoodMediaCommunications.com creates all customized Thank You, Note Cards, Invitation and any other type of stationary you may need.

3. Join the blogging community on BabyCenter.com.

CHAPTER 7

1. www.babycenter.com

2. www.kangaroomothercare.com

3. www.SendOutCards.com/27556

4. www.winsorpilates.com

5. www.gaiam.com

6. www.anonymousone.com

CHAPTER 8

1. Baby Signing Time: Available at www.signingtime.com

2. Baby Einstein: My First Signs: Available at Amazon. com

3. Wee Hands. Visit www.weehands.com to sign-up for a class near you.

4. Baby Signing Time: Available at www.signingtime.com

5. Baby Einstein: My First Signs: Available at Amazon. com

6. Wee Hands. Visit www.weehands.com to sign-up for a class near you.

CHAPTER 9

1. www.michaelolaf.com provides a wealth of information and practical life materials for parents and teachers to help their toddler learn independence and self-care.

CHAPTER 10

1. Shaklee makes wonderful non-toxic, eco-friendly household, laundry and kitchen cleaners that are biodegradable and safe for the earth, your babies and your entire family. Available at www.shaklee.net/ sortedout.

2. California Baby offers an extensive line of all natural products for the natural baby. From full body care to essential oils, totes and accessories, this online boutique has it all! www.californiababy.com.

3. Visit http://community.gaiam.com/ for more information about eco-living.

4. Freecycle.org is a fantastic Web site to dispose of items you no longer need, as well as to obtain items (for free) that you may need.

FORMS

PARTNERSHIP PLAN

The purpose of the Partnership Plan is to form a commitment between you and your spouse to fairly and lovingly assign specific household chores to one another. As you create your partnership plan, keep in mind the division of labor can and should be revisited as your lives evolve and change.

DAILY CHILD CARE

Duty	Monday	Tuesday	Wednesday	Thursday	Friday	Saturday	Sunday
Early Morning Feedings							
Late Night Feedings							
Morning Bottle Prep.							
Late Night Bottle Prep.							

DAILY HOUSEHOLD CLEANUP

Duty	Monday	Tuesday	Wednesday	Thursday	Friday	Saturday	Sunday
Kitchen Cleanup							
morning							
noon							
evening							
Laundry							
children's							
adult							
Beds							
children's							
adults							
Meal Prep.							
breakfast							
lunch							
snack							
dinner							

PARTNERSHIP PLAN

The purpose of the Partnership Plan is to form a commitment between you and your spouse to fairly and lovingly assign specific household chores to one another. As you create your partnership plan, keep in mind the division of labor can and should be revisited as your lives evolve and change.

WEEKLY HOUSE-HOLD CLEANUP	Duty	Monday	Tuesday	Wednesday	Thursday	Friday	Saturday	Sunday
	Lawn Care							
	Pool Care							
	Grocery Shopping							

Special Considerations
Should we hire a housekeeper? If so, how many days per month should he or she work?

_____

_____

_____

_____

Discuss your current professional work schedule. Are there adjustments that need to be made with regard to the number of hours worked or the amount of travel required?

_____

_____

_____

_____

Will one parent stay home with the children long-term? How will this impact the division of labor?

_____

_____

_____

_____

Will you hire a nanny? What will her household responsibilities entail?

_____

_____

_____

_____

If you will be utilizing daycare, who will drop off and pick up?

_____

_____

_____

_____

Do you have friends or family that will be willing to help out regularly?

_____

_____

_____

_____

FAMILY CORE VALUES

The purpose of the Family Core Values form is to commit on paper what you and your spouse agree will be the core governing principles of your family. Your core values should be what structures every important family decision. You should be able to ask yourselves prior to making a decision: Will this support our family's core values? A simple yes or no answer to that question should be all you need to move forward with your decision.

Your family's core values should ...

- Govern your personal inter-family relationships
- Guide your home processes
- Clarify who you are as a family unit
- Articulate what you stand for as a family
- Be a parental guide for teaching your children
- Be a parental guide for rewarding your children
- Provide a moral foundation for the family

Together, with your spouse or any other children who may currently reside within the family, develop a two to three sentence statement for each of the following prompts:

Our family will hold the following virtues as the guiding principle for all inter-family relationships:

_____

_____

_____

_____

The following principles will be the foundation of all our home processes:

_____

_____

_____

_____

As a family, we will continuously strive to be:

_____

_____

_____

_____

As a family, we will make a stand for our most sacred truths, which are as follows:

_____

_____

_____

_____

FAMILY CORE VALUES

The purpose of the Family Core Values form is to commit on paper what you and your spouse agree will be the core governing principles of your family. Your core values should be what structures every important family decision. You should be able to ask yourselves prior to making a decision: Will this support our family's core values? A simple yes or no answer to that question should be all you need to move forward with your decision.

As parents, we agree to support one another in our effort to educate and morally guide our children by implementing the following method of discipline:

_____
_____
_____
_____

As parents, we agree to support one another in our effort to educate and morally guide our children by implementing the following reward system:

_____
_____
_____
_____

As parents, we promise one another that we will mutually commit to providing the following moral foundation for our children:

_____
_____
_____
_____

Additional:

_____
_____
_____
_____
_____
_____
_____
_____
_____
_____
_____

SIGN UP TO ASSIST

Use the Sign Up To Assist form to ensure you have ample help on hand when your babies arrive.

DAILY HOUSEHOLD CLEANUP

Time	Monday	Tuesday	Wednesday	Thursday	Friday	Saturday	Sunday
7:00 am							
7:30 am							
8:00 am							
8:30 am							
9:00 am							
9:30 am							
10:00 am							
10:30 am							
11:00 am							
11:30 am							
12:00 pm							
12:30 pm							
1:00 pm							
1:30 pm							
2:00 pm							
2:30 pm							
3:00 pm							
3:30 pm							
4:00 pm							
4:30 pm							
5:00 pm							
5:30 pm							
6:00 pm							
6:30 pm							
7:00 pm							

SAMPLE LETTER

Your Name
Your Address
Your City, State, Zip
Your Email

Date

Name
Address
City, State, Zip

To Whom It May Concern:

Please find enclosed copies of our twins' birth certificates. We know you can imagine the cost involved with having twins and we appreciate any complimentary products your company may be able to offer. We would also appreciate any coupons, so we can purchase your goods in the future.

Sincerely,

Your Name Here

SAMPLE BUDGET
MONTHLY EXPENSES

PERSONAL CARE	MONTHLY COST	KITCHEN	MONTHLY COST	BATHROOM	MONTHLY COST
	$		$		$
	$		$		$
	$		$		$
	$		$		$
	$		$		$
	$		$		$
	$		$		$
	$		$		$
	$		$		$
	$		$		$
	$		$		$
	$		$		$
	$		$		$
	$		$		$
	$		$		$
	$		$		$
	$		$		$
	$		$		$
	$		$		$
	$		$		$
	$		$		$
	$		$		$
	$		$		$
	$		$		$
	$		$		$
SUB TOTALS:	$	+	$	+	$
=					
TOTAL	$	X 36 MONTHS =		GRAND TOTAL	$

PERSONAL CARE	ONE-TIME COST	KITCHEN	ONE-TIME COST	BATHROOM	ONE-TIME COST
SUB TOTALS	$	+	$	+	$
=					
TOTAL A	$				

CAR	ONE-TIME COST	NURSERY	ONE-TIME COST	PLAY STATIONS	ONE-TIME COST
SUB TOTALS	$	+	$	+	$
=					
TOTAL B	$				

TRAVEL	ONE-TIME COST	SAFETY	ONE-TIME COST
SUB TOTALS	$	+	$
=			
TOTAL C	$	A+B+C= GRAND TOTAL	$

Monthly Exp Grand Total*	$
One Time Exp Grand Total	+ $
Grand Total	= $
Singleton Cost	$
Twin Cost	$
Triplet Cost	$
Quad Cost	$
Quint Cost	$

Please note, Monthly Expense Grand Total is based on 36 months.

GIFT INFORMATION
& THANK YOU

	Date	Description of Gift	From	Thank You Card Sent
BABY SHOWER THANK YOU				

GIFT INFORMATION
& THANK YOU

SIP & SEE THANK YOU

Date	Description of Gift	From	Thank You Card Sent

GIFT INFORMATION
& THANK YOU

	Date	Description of Gift	From	Thank You Card Sent
CHRISTENING THANK YOU				

REGISTRY CHECKLIST

CHAOS 2 CALM

PERSONAL CARE

ITEM	QUANTITY PER BABY	RECEIVED	STILL NEED	GIVEN BY	THANK YOU NOTE SENT
Diapers					
Wipes					
Diaper Rash Cream					
Mylicon					
Breast Pump					
Pacifiers					
Pain Reliever Medicine					
First Aid Kit					
Humidifier					
Body Support Pillow					
milk storage bags					

KITCHEN

ITEM	QUANTITY PER BABY	RECEIVED	STILL NEED	GIVEN BY	THANK YOU NOTE SENT
Bottle					
Bottle Warmer					
Sterilizer					
Sippy Cups					
Flatware/Cutlery					
Plates/Bowls					
Bottle Drying Rack					
Bottle Brush					
Cabinet Locks					
Bibs					

CAR

ITEM	QUANTITY PER BABY	RECEIVED	STILL NEED	GIVEN BY	THANK YOU NOTE SENT
Infant Seat					
Toddler					
Roller Shade					
Car Mirror					
Seat Saver					

NURSERY

ITEM	QUANTITY PER BABY	RECEIVED	STILL NEED	GIVEN BY	THANK YOU NOTE SENT
Crib					
Nursery Chair					
Changing Table					
Crib Sheets					
WATERPROOF MATTRESS PAD					
Clothing					
Sheet Protector					
Closet Size Organizer					
Hangers					
Blankets					
Chair Table					

BATHROOM

ITEM	QUANTITY PER BABY	RECEIVED	STILL NEED	GIVEN BY	THANK YOU NOTE SENT
Spout Cover					
Towels					
Wash Cloths					
Tub					
Tub Toys					
Shower Curtain					
Bath Mat					

TRAVEL

ITEM	QUANTITY PER BABY	RECEIVED	STILL NEED	GIVEN BY	THANK YOU NOTE SENT
Stroller					
Bjourn					
Diaper Bag					
Swaddler					
Pack and Play					

APPLICANT INFORMATION

Name

Address

City

State

Zip Code

Phone Number

Fax Number

Email

Education

High School	College
Address	Address
Did you graduate?	Did you graduate?
Date	Date
Degree	Degree
Email	Email

Additional Education

Special Skills

Previous Employment

Name of Employer	Dates of Employment
Reason for leaving	Position
Duties/Responsibilities	

Name of Employer	Dates of Employment
Reason for leaving	Position
Duties/Responsibilities	

Name of Employer	Dates of Employment
Reason for leaving	Position
Duties/Responsibilities	

CAREGIVER APPLICATION

CHAOS 2 CALM

CAREGIVER APPLICATION

CHAOS 2 CALM

Name	Name
Address	Address
City	City
State	State
Zip Code	Zip Code
Phone Number	Phone Number
Relationship	Relationship
Years of Acquaintance	Years of Acquaintance

Name	Name
Address	Address
City	City
State	State
Zip Code	Zip Code
Phone Number	Phone Number
Relationship	Relationship
Years of Acquaintance	Years of Acquaintance

Name	Name
Address	Address
City	City
State	State
Zip Code	Zip Code
Phone Number	Phone Number
Relationship	Relationship
Years of Acquaintance	Years of Acquaintance

By signing below, you agree that all of the information in this application is true to the full extent of your knowledge.

_____   _____
Applicant   Date

Customer Information

Name

Address

City

State

Zip Code

Phone Number

Fax Number

Email

Child Care Provider Information

Name

Address

City

State

Zip Code

Phone Number

Fax Number

Email

Children's Information

Name	Name
Birth Date	Birth Date
Name	Name
Birth Date	Birth Date

special notes:

Description of services to be provided:

The Customer hereby agrees to engage Child Care Provider to provide the Customer with the following services:

Duties and tasks both parties agree on as outlined below:

Terms of Agreement

This agreement becomes effective on the following date: _____
and will remain in effect until either party provides a fourteen day written notice of termination or resignation.

CAREGIVER AGREEMENT FORM

CHAOS
2 CALM

Hourly

Weekly

Monthly

Fixed Rate

Per Child Rate

Additional Compensation

Child Care Provider Confidence Agreement

By signing this document the Child Care Provider agrees to hold in confidence all of

Customer's personal family matters including:

Customer

Date

Child Care Provider

Date

CAREGIVER AGREEMENT FORM

CHAOS
2 CALM

Child Care Provider Hours

| Monday |
| Tuesday |
| Wednesday |
| Thursday |
| Friday |
| Saturday |
| Sunday |

Sick Day Policy
List the number of sick days allowed per calendar year. Indicate whether or not these days are paid or unpaid. Indicate whether not these days rollover to the following calendar year. Note the call-in policy for utilizing sick days.

_____

_____

_____

Personal Day Policy
List the number of personal days allowed per calendar year. Indicate whether or not these days are paid or unpaid. Indicate whether not these days rollover to the following calendar year. Note the call-in policy for utilizing personal days.

_____

_____

_____

Tardy or No-Show Policy
Indicate your policy regarding tardiness or "no-showing."
How will these situations be dealt with.

_____

_____

_____

Policy Regarding Bringing Children To Work
May your child care provider bring his or her own children to work? If, so, what are the stipulations regarding this policy?

_____

_____

_____

Additional

_____

_____

_____

Child Care Provider Job Description

Hours Responsibilities Shall Be Performed

Monday

Tuesday

Wednesday

Thursday

Friday

Saturday

Sunday

Primary Responsibilities

Secondary Responsibilities

Tertiary Responsibilities

Additional Responsibilities

CHILD CARE PROVIDER DAILY TO-DO LIST

Time	
7:00 am	
7:30 am	
8:00 am	
8:30 am	
9:00 am	
9:30 am	
10:00 am	
10:30 am	
11:00 am	
11:30 am	
12:00 pm	
12:30 pm	
1:00 pm	
1:30 pm	
2:00 pm	
2:30 pm	
3:00 pm	
3:30 pm	
4:00 pm	
4:30 pm	
5:00 pm	
5:30 pm	
6:00 pm	
6:30 pm	
7:00 pm	

EMERGENCY CONTACT NUMBERS

Emergency   911

Poison Control

Non-Emergency

Non-Emergency

Fire Department

Police Department

Home Address

Address

City

State

Zip Code

Phone Number

Mom Full Name	Dad Full Name
Cell Phone	Cell Phone
Business Phone	Business Phone
Email	Email
Other	Other

Pediatrician	Emergency Pediatrician
Address	Address
City	City
State	State
Zip Code	Zip Code
Phone Number	Phone Number

Veterinarian	Emergency Veterinarian
Address	Address
City	City
State	State
Zip Code	Zip Code
Phone Number	Phone Number

Grandparent 1	Grandparent 2
Address	Address
City	City
State	State
Zip Code	Zip Code
Phone Number	Phone Number
Cell Phone	Cell Phone

EMERGENCY CONTACT NUMBERS

CHAOS
2 CALM

Grandparent 3	Grandparent 4
Address	Address
City	City
State	State
Zip Code	Zip Code
Phone Number	Phone Number
Cell Phone	Cell Phone

Neighbor 1	Neighbor 2
Address	Address
City	City
State	State
Zip Code	Zip Code
Phone Number	Phone Number
Cell Phone	Cell Phone

Neighbor 3	Neighbor 4
Address	Address
City	City
State	State
Zip Code	Zip Code
Phone Number	Phone Number
Cell Phone	Cell Phone

School 1	School 2
Address	Address
City	City
State	State
Zip Code	Zip Code
Phone Number	Phone Number
Teacher Number	Teacher Number

Other Contact 1	Other Contact 2
Address	Address
City	City
State	State
Zip Code	Zip Code
Phone Number	Phone Number
Cell Phone	Cell Phone

MEDICATION ADMINISTRATION FORM

1. Medication shall only be administered by _____
   (name of child care provider) under the direction of a Medical Administration Form.

2. Medication will always be in its original, childproof container.

3. Medication must always be stored out of the reach of all children.

Prescription Medication

Medication shall be administered in accordance with the pharmacy label directions as prescribed by the child's health care provider.

Non-Prescription (Over-the-Counter) Medications

1. May be administered only under the direction of parent and must be accompanied with a signed Medical Administration Form.

2. Non-prescription medication shall be administered in accordance with the product label directions on the container.

Authorization for Medication Administration

I hereby authorize (name of authorized agent): _____
to administer the following medication to my child (name of child)

Parent/Guardian Name _____
Phone Number _____
Health Care Provider _____
Phone Number _____
Purpose of Medication is _____

Time of Administration: _____
Time of Administration: _____
Time of Administration: _____
Time of Administration: _____

Name of Medication: _____
Method of Administration: _____
Possible Side Effects: _____
In case of an emergency contact: _____
Phone Number: _____

Parent/Guardian Signature _____
Today's Date: _____

ALLERGY & OTHER MEDICAL INFORMATION

Name

Blood Type

Social Security Number

Medicinal Allergies

Food Allergies

Medical Conditions

Allergy & Other Medical Information

Name

Blood Type

Social Security Number

Medicinal Allergies

Food Allergies

Medical Conditions

TELEVISION & MOVIE POLICY

List of networks children are allowed to view.

_____

_____

_____

_____

List of shows children are allowed to view.

_____

_____

_____

_____

List of shows/movies/networks children are never allowed to view.

_____

_____

_____

_____

Number of hours per day children may view television.

_____

_____

_____

Particular times children are allowed to view television.

7:00 am	1:30 pm
7:30 am	2:00 pm
8:00 am	2:30 pm
8:30 am	3:00 pm
9:00 am	3:30 pm
9:30 am	4:00 pm
10:00 am	4:30 pm
10:30 am	5:00 pm
11:00 am	5:30 pm
11:30 am	6:00 pm
12:00 pm	6:30 pm
12:30 pm	7:00 pm
1:00 pm	7:30 pm

POOL POLICY

Pool Supervision Policy. Indicate your policy regarding supervision.

Friends Swimming Policy. Indicate your policy regarding having friends over for swimming (nanny's and children's).

Pool Snacks & Refreshments Policy. Indicate your policy regarding food and beverages near pool (nanny's and children's).

Pool Alarm Codes

Number of hours per day children may swim per day.

Particular times children are allowed to swim.

7:00 am	1:30 pm
7:30 am	2:00 pm
8:00 am	2:30 pm
8:30 am	3:00 pm
9:00 am	3:30 pm
9:30 am	4:00 pm
10:00 am	4:30 pm
10:30 am	5:00 pm
11:00 am	5:30 pm
11:30 am	6:00 pm
12:00 pm	6:30 pm
12:30 pm	7:00 pm
1:00 pm	7:30 pm

ACTIVITY SCHEDULE

7:00 am

7:30 am

8:00 am

8:30 am

9:00 am

9:30 am

10:00 am

10:30 am

11:00 am

11:30 am

12:00 pm

12:30 pm

1:00 pm

1:30 pm

2:00 pm

2:30 pm

3:00 pm

3:30 pm

4:00 pm

4:30 pm

5:00 pm

5:30 pm

6:00 pm

6:30 pm

7:00 pm

DAYCARE SHOPPING GUIDE

Daycare Shopping Guide

1. Compile a list of daycare centers based on referrals you have received from your pediatrician, friends, family and personal research.

2. Search the Internet for Child Protective Services for your state. This state agency will log all reports of state regulatory non-compliance for every licensed daycare center, as well as licensed home care providers. Make notes about the facilities that interest you. Please note, it is rare for facility to receive a perfect score at every state agency observation. Do not eliminate a facility based on a few of non-compliances; however you should do additional research to determine the severity of the non-compliance and the circumstances surrounding the non-compliance.

3. Call to schedule a tour of the daycare. Do not drop by unannounced on your first visit. Some centers only provide tours on specific days and times. While some centers will tour "drop-ins," you do not want to be rushed through the tour or be asked to wait for a long period while the administrator finishes his or her task at hand. Remember, she has a job to do outside of being the center tour guide. Be polite and call ahead. You will have a much better experience.

4. Notes:

_____

_____

_____

_____

_____

_____

_____

_____

_____

_____

_____

_____

_____

_____

_____

_____

_____

_____

_____

Rank this facility from 1 to 10 with 10 being the highest ranking:

Facility Name

Address

Phone Number

Web site

Tour Date

Tour Notes

Rank this facility from 1 to 10 with 10 being the highest ranking:

Facility Name

Address

Phone Number

Web site

Tour Date

Tour Notes

Rank this facility from 1 to 10 with 10 being the highest ranking:

Facility Name

Address

Phone Number

Web site

Tour Date

Tour Notes

DAYCARE SHOPPING GUIDE

CHAOS
2 CALM

TOP THREE
DAYCARE
SHOPPING GUIDE

After touring all of the centers on your Daycare Shopping Guide, use your ranking system to narrow your selections to the top three.

The second visit is when you "drop-in" without notice. Let the administrator know that you do not need to occupy her time but simply that you would like to observe one or several of the classrooms quietly for 30 minutes. Make notes on your form to review later.

During your observation note the following:

Facility Name: _____

Administrator Name: _____

Phone Number: _____

1. How many teachers are in the classroom you observed? Is the classroom within the state required student to teacher ratio (you can find this information on your local child protective services Web site)?

_____
_____
_____

2. Are the teachers courteous to the children?

_____
_____
_____

3. Are the teachers talking with the children or with each other?

_____
_____
_____

4. Do the children seem happy? Are they clean?

_____
_____
_____

5. Is the classroom organized and clean?

_____
_____
_____

6. Does the room smell nice or like a diaper pail?

_____

_____

_____

7. Is the classroom structured to be child-friendly, or teacher-friendly?

_____

_____

_____

8. Are the teachers uncomfortable with your presence?

_____

_____

_____

Additional notes and observations:

_____

_____

_____

_____

_____

_____

_____

On a scale of one to ten, how do you rank this facility based on your second observation?

_____

_____

_____

_____

_____

_____

_____

COMMUNICATION LOG

Date:

From Parent:

_____
_____
_____
_____
_____
_____
_____
_____
_____
_____
_____
_____
_____

Date:

From Child Care Provider:

_____
_____
_____
_____
_____
_____
_____
_____
_____
_____
_____
_____
_____

FEEDING SCHEDULE

CHAOS 2 CALM

	Feedings/Diapers									
	1	2	3	4	5	6	7	8	9	
Targeted Time	7:00 am	10:00 am	1:00 pm	4:00 pm	7:00 pm					TOTALS
Actual Time										
Monday	R=	R=	R=	R=	R=					
Date: ___/___/___	L=	L=	L=	L=	L=					
R= Right Breast L= Left Breast	#Wet	#Wet	#Wet	#Wet	#Wet	#Wet	#Wet	#Wet		
	#Poop	#Poop	#Poop	#Poop	#Poop	#Poop	#Poop	#Poop		
Targeted Time	7:00 am	10:00 am	1:00 pm	4:00 pm	7:00 pm					TOTALS
Actual Time										
Tuesday	R=	R=	R=	R=	R=					
Date: ___/___/___	L=	L=	L=	L=	L=					
R= Right Breast L= Left Breast	#Wet	#Wet	#Wet	#Wet	#Wet	#Wet	#Wet	#Wet		
	#Poop	#Poop	#Poop	#Poop	#Poop	#Poop	#Poop	#Poop		
Targeted Time	7:00 am	10:00 am	1:00 pm	4:00 pm	7:00 pm					TOTALS
Actual Time										
Wednesday	R=	R=	R=	R=	R=					
Date: ___/___/___	L=	L=	L=	L=	L=					
R= Right Breast L= Left Breast	#Wet	#Wet	#Wet	#Wet	#Wet	#Wet	#Wet	#Wet		
	#Poop	#Poop	#Poop	#Poop	#Poop	#Poop	#Poop	#Poop		
Targeted Time	7:00 am	10:00 am	1:00 pm	4:00 pm	7:00 pm					TOTALS
Actual Time										
Thursday	R=	R=	R=	R=	R=					
Date: ___/___/___	L=	L=	L=	L=	L=					
R= Right Breast L= Left Breast	#Wet	#Wet	#Wet	#Wet	#Wet	#Wet	#Wet	#Wet		
	#Poop	#Poop	#Poop	#Poop	#Poop	#Poop	#Poop	#Poop		
Targeted Time	7:00 am	10:00 am	1:00 pm	4:00 pm	7:00 pm					TOTALS
Actual Time										
Friday	R=	R=	R=	R=	R=					
Date: ___/___/___	L=	L=	L=	L=	L=					
R= Right Breast L= Left Breast	#Wet	#Wet	#Wet	#Wet	#Wet	#Wet	#Wet	#Wet		
	#Poop	#Poop	#Poop	#Poop	#Poop	#Poop	#Poop	#Poop		
Targeted Time	7:00 am	10:00 am	1:00 pm	4:00 pm	7:00 pm					TOTALS
Actual Time										
Saturday	R=	R=	R=	R=	R=					
Date: ___/___/___	L=	L=	L=	L=	L=					
R= Right Breast L= Left Breast	#Wet	#Wet	#Wet	#Wet	#Wet	#Wet	#Wet	#Wet		
	#Poop	#Poop	#Poop	#Poop	#Poop	#Poop	#Poop	#Poop		
Targeted Time	7:00 am	10:00 am	1:00 pm	4:00 pm	7:00 pm					TOTALS
Actual Time										
Sunday	R=	R=	R=	R=	R=					
Date: ___/___/___	L=	L=	L=	L=	L=					
R= Right Breast L= Left Breast	#Wet	#Wet	#Wet	#Wet	#Wet	#Wet	#Wet	#Wet		
	#Poop	#Poop	#Poop	#Poop	#Poop	#Poop	#Poop	#Poop		

Index

A

Activity Schedule 69, 70, 87, 120, 189
Allergy & Medical Information
  Allergy 69, 73, 84, 172
  Medical 16, 69, 84, 172
    Medication Administration 83, 171

B

Baby Placement 31
Bath 4, 39, 40, 53
  Bathrooms 39, 53
  Faucet Cover 40, 53
Bed Rest 97-99
Blind Cords 48
Borrowing 11
Breastfeeding 103
  Kangaroo Care 103
Budget 7, 9, 10, 17, 25-28, 154-157

C

Cabinets 40, 47, 50, 53
Changing Station 34, 35, 36, 42, 105
  Changing Table 34-36, 106
  Changing Zone 34
  Diaper Changing 105
Closet 32, 38
Communication Center 41
  Communications 92, 117, 180
Crib Tent II 53

D

Daily Activity Form 69, 87, 120, 175
Daily To-Do List 70, 80, 168
Date Night 2, 3, 17, 78
Daycare 6, 20, 71-72
  Daycare Shopping Guide 88-91,
    176-179
Diapers 14, 17, 34, 38, 42, 105,
    107-109, 116, 130, 131, 132,
    135-137, 139
Diaper Changing 34, 105, 108, 139
Diet 7, 70, 127-129
Doctor 7, 16, 97-98, 104, 110
Doorstops 49

E

Eco-baby 127-133
Electrical Outlets 48
Emergency Contact Numbers 69, 81-82
Employee Handbook 69

F

Family Core Values 6, 21-22, 150-151
Family Room 41
Fire Drill
  Fire Escape Ladder 46
  Fire Extinguishers 47
Fireplace 49
First Aid Kits 47, 137
Food Safety
  Freezer Fresh 51

Forms 19-29, 61-64, 112, 119-120, 147
  Baby Shower 61
  Christening 63
  Daily To-Do List 80
  Feeding & Activity Schedule 87, 119
  Partnership Plan 19-20
  Request For Samples Letter 24
  Shower Registry Checklist 64
  Sign-Up to Assist 23
  Sip & See Gift Form 62
  Thank You 61-64
  Top Three Daycare Observation form 90-91
  TV Policy Form 85
Freebies 17, 142
Freecycle.org 32, 130, 145
Furniture Wall Straps 48

G
Gates 49

H
Homecoming 59, 101
Hospital 8, 16, 31, 55, 96-99
  Hospital Bags 96, 103

I
International Association For Child Safety 54, 143
Invitations 60, 143

J
Journaling 1-2, 4, 17, 97, 101

K
Kitchen
  Ground Fault 50

L
Lid Lock 53

M
Mothers of Multiples 10
Mothers of Supertwins 10, 18, 142
MyPRO Health Records Organizer
  Mommy & Babies Medical Binder 16
MyPRO Interior Design Organizer
  Interior Design Organizer 32

N
Nanny 6, 67-71, 138, 144
  Job Description 70, 79
  Nanny Book 69, 71
National Mothers of Twins Club 10
Nesting 57, 95-96
Notes 97
Nursery 31-34
  Nursery Storage 38

O

Organic 9, 129-132
  Baby Food 129-130
  Fashion 130

P

Partnership Plan 19
Play Zone 33, 36, 42
Pool 71
  Pool Policy 86
Premature baby 104

R

Request For Samples Letter 24

S

Saf-er-Grip 53
Safety 39, 40, 47-49, 54, 136
Sample Products 12
Shoe Labels 38
Shower Registry Checklist 64
Sign-Up To Assist 23
Sleeping Zone 33
  Sleep-Time Positioner 33
Smoke Alarms 46

T

Take Out Menu Organizer 40
The Twins Network 11
Toilet lock 53
Top Three Daycare Observation Form 90-91
Travel 135, 138-140
TV Policy Form 85

QUICK ORDER FORM

Fax Orders: 972-985-7515

Telephone Orders: 972-985-7515

Email Orders: Orders@momsofmultiplesguide.com

Postal Orders: Sorted Out™
Chaos 2 Calm
2124 Deerfield Drive
Plano TX 75023

Yes! I would like to order _____ copies
of *Chaos 2 Calm: the moms-of-multiples'
guide to an organized family.*

Please send me information regarding:

☐ Consulting

☐ Speaking Engagements

☐ Organizational Services

$17.95

Name: _____

Address: _____

City: _____

State: _____   Zip: _____

Telephone: _____

Email: _____

Sales Tax: Please add the 8.25% sales tax for products shipped to Texas.

*Shipping by air: U.S.: $4.00 for the first book and $2.00 for each additional
product. International: $9.00 for first book; $5.00 for each additional book.*

QUICK ORDER FORM

Fax Orders: 972-985-7515

Telephone Orders: 972-985-7515

Email Orders: Orders@momsofmultiplesguide.com

Postal Orders: Sorted Out™
Chaos 2 Calm
2124 Deerfield Drive
Plano TX 75023

Yes! I would like to order _____ copies
of *Chaos 2 Calm: the moms-of-multiples'
guide to an organized family.*

Please send me information regarding:

☐ Consulting

☐ Speaking Engagements

☐ Organizational Services

$17.95

Name: _____

Address: _____

City: _____

State: _____ Zip: _____

Telephone: _____

Email: _____

Sales Tax: Please add the 8.25% sales tax for products shipped to Texas.

*Shipping by air: U.S.: $4.00 for the first book and $2.00 for each additional
product. International: $9.00 for first book; $5.00 for each additional book.*